# TEXTURES OF LIFE

# TEXTURES OF LIFE

*Walking Through Your Pain*

JERRE NORTHINGTON

Book designer and Photographer: Designs by Valentine LLC - Christopher Valentine

Editor: Danielle Rouse

ISBN: 9798218070236
Published by Jerre Northington
Publisher Consultant Sophisticated Press

# ACKNOWLEDGMENTS

I am because he was. Daddy, you will forever live in my heart. You are the reason I'm a cosmetologist. I miss you so much. Cheers to you, and I know you are so proud of me. While I wish I could see your face and you could see me accomplish my life's goals, I can feel you. I know that you, Big Granma, and Nita are watching over me.

To my mom, siblings, and family members, who encouraged me to keep going. To those who helped me understand that my story could help so many people. When it was dark for me, you became my light. Thank you!

To Danielle Rouse, my editor and friend. She pushed me to an uncomfortable place, even when life got challenging, and my vision changed. I'm so grateful for that.

To Angela, Lisa, Ivory, Miama, Kristen, Kendra, and Christen, these women showed up for my children. They took care of my children as their own. I will forever be grateful for the time they gave to my family. Thank you for your love and prayers.

Coach Ro offered valuable tips on creating authentic, valuable content that would help motivate and empower people. She has been a part of my life for 20-plus years. She gives tough love to push you to your highest potential. Always willing to take a few minutes to encourage me. Thank you for giving it to me straight.

To my brother Garry, who always filled the void. Although he is a very busy man these days, he will still find time to nurture the children of the family—a true man of God-loving husband and father. I appreciate and love you so much.

To my N'Style Family, thank you for the constant prayers, support, and encouragement through all of my life transitions. A special thank you to Nate. I am forever grateful to you.

My family, *The J clan*, you guys are my rock. I carry the hugs and long late-night conversations with you guys with me. Your words of encouragement have kept me, no matter how challenging times have been. I am so proud to be your mom.

# Table of Contents

# CHAPTER 1

# Summers at Big Granma's

Scorching days like this make me want to jump in a pool. My body might be in shock at first, but I'll adjust quickly to the cold temperature. Someone is grilling in the neighborhood. I can smell the charcoal. Hear the ice cream truck. Taste a refreshing orange creamsicle. The fire hydrant opens up, and the water looks like the opening of a shaken soda can. Summers like this remind me of my childhood.

My siblings and I are packed and ready for summer weekends with Big Granma. Most people say Grandma with a D, but we say Granma. She lives in a one-bedroom apartment on the third floor. When we come over, Big Granma always makes sure we eat good. Fried fish, okra, black-eyed peas, liver, and gravy with onions are staples on our plates. We enjoy going to the wharf with her to get a bushel of live crabs. We would help her put them in the pot when we got home. Now and then, one or two escapes, and Big Granma has to chase them. Sometimes we chase them for fun. Watching us try to catch them crabs and not get pinched always makes Big Granma chuckle.

She taught us how to make a palette of sheets and blankets to sleep comfortably on the floor. In the mornings, we fold our blankets and eat breakfast. Two breakfast favorites are scrapple and grits or oatmeal and sausage. Most of the time, we mix the meat into the hot cereal. We watch cartoons until it's time for Big Granma's shows and, eventually, the news. Her T.V is about 24 inches and has two nodes on the upper right side. When you turn the knobs, it clicks to one of four channels: 4, 5, 7, and 20. If the antenna isn't positioned correctly, it doesn't work. We are never allowed to change her channel, but sometimes we would without her noticing.

There's a daybed in her living room. A table of trinkets collected from cleaning apartments is to the right. She didn't like for us to play with her things. Most of them are old-school McDonald's toys, so it's hard not to touch them. My favorite is this tiny little bear. Very very small--the size of the tip of a pinky finger. We found it sweeping out an apartment. Big Granma's job is to clean apartments after tenants move out, and I often go along to help her. While she swept, I was picking up the big pieces of trash when she stopped me and told me to pick it up. I always do the bending for her, but I couldn't see it in the mound of trash. "Girl, get that bear; it's right there." I pushed the debris around, and there it was. So cute and tiny, a porcelain dark brown teddy bear wearing a red bow tie. One of her trinkets is a turtle. It looks like the rubber duckies for the bathtub, but she treasured it for being unique because it's a turtle. When I was younger, she let me play with it while I took a bath, but she always told me to play quietly so my siblings wouldn't see.

Big Granma is a beautiful dark skin woman with long silver curly hair, and I grease, brush, braid it, and sometimes give her Bantu knots. She asks me to come run errands, like accompanying her to the grocery store and doctor's appointments, so I can read and write for her. She couldn't write a signature and would always sign with an x. Although my mom, in junior high, taught her to write her name, I still helped her. My siblings think I am Big Granma's favorite, so I'm the one to ask when they want something. I always sneak to get the candy she hides under her pillow on the daybed. I help wash her back and shampoo her hair when she takes her baths.

Summer weekends with Big Granma shaped me. I didn't realize it then, but she was my very first client teaching me how to detangle hair. After 23 years in the cosmetology industry, I still use her detangling method. After a shampoo and condition, I gently separate the hair into manageable sections, starting at the ends with my comb and working my way to the scalp. It's muscle memory.

My grandmother and her seven siblings were born enslaved on Porter Farm in Texas. She picked cotton until she started working in the kitchen at three years old. She was so tiny that she had to stand on a box to wash dishes. She openly told us stories of her childhood but never discussed her life as a teenager. She just said it was hard and didn't want to stay there.

In her twenties, she moved to Washington, D.C, to live with her brother Sam. He is the youngest boy, and she is the youngest girl. They are very close, even though they are eight years apart. Big Granma may have left Texas because there was more money for jobs or because she was accused of committing a crime. A man tried to sexually assault her, and she defended herself. Her family rushed her away to protect her. Shortly after, she decided to move to D.C. and to this day says she don't have time for "menfolk." We still don't know the whole story.

After Sam retired from the service, he opened his own business, and his wife was a hairdresser. She helped Big Granma get her first job laying the tracks on a railroad. Since Big Granma has only a third-grade education, her sister-in-law took the entry assessment. Big Granma wanted her sister-in-law to take the test because she was light-skinned and educated. The questions were basic reading comprehension, math skills, and a personality test. Big Granma secured and kept the job without her employer knowing she could not read.

My mother's dad was an alcoholic, and although Big Granma loved him, she chose not to marry him. Uncle Sam helped care for my mother as a child while Big Granma worked; he was her only father figure. My mom was two years old when Big Granma contracted tuberculosis from her primary care physician. After three years of hospitalization, she regained her strength, but her doctor did not survive. Big Granma never lets anything slow her down, and I admire her fighter spirit. She continuously supports us with her love and wisdom.

I remember one year Big Granma's sisters and cousins came to visit. Her apartment was plenty of room for all of us. I sat at the table watching three beautiful, strong black women move around in her tiny kitchen area. It was like watching a well-practiced dance routine. Everyone knew what to do, when to move over, and help one another out. Their synergy produced a delicious breakfast for all the grandkids and family members visiting.

I have always had a similar synergy when creating hairstyles, which translates to each individual sitting in my chair. I remember having my elbow on my leg and my hand on my chin, watching my mom create cornrows for my sisters Theresa, Sierra, and Faniesha before it was my turn. I would mimic what her hands were doing, and by the time I was a preteen, I was doing my hair and Faniesha's too. I could look at the hairstyles in *Hype Magazine* and recreate them easily. The first style I tried out was the Missy Elliott finger waves. It was my first piece of hair art. What I did then became a platform for my career as a cosmetologist. My clients can show me a picture, and I can recreate it or recreate it with my unique twist.

Clients love getting their hair styled, but taking styles out can be daunting and challenging. There may be product build-up, dry scalp, or dead hair waiting to fall depending on the client's hair care routine, their approach to taking the style down, and how long they have kept the hairstyle.

Use a conditioner to soften the hair and allow dead hair to fall away quickly. With braids, it is best to start at the ends with a rat tail comb and move slowly up the braid. Be sure to pay attention when pulling the braid entirely apart at the ends. This limits tangles. This same technique can be applied when navigating life's obstacles. Take a moment to assess where you are. Understand what you need to overcome. Take one step at a time to work out the kinks. Then, you can choose to move forward with ease. Trust me. I've had to persevere through so many obstacles in my life.

There are four hair textures. On one end is straight hair, which has no movement. The straight hair texture is comparable to the well-mapped-out beginning phases of life. I had a routine I picked up from my older siblings as a child. Wake up, groom myself and fix my breakfast. I learned to be mindful of the time to catch the morning school bus. There was a school day routine and the evening routine of homework, dinner, and chores before bed. Although there are ways to change the shape of straight hair, it always returns to its natural form. Similarly, the first phase of life was straightforward, with a routine that rarely changed.

The second hair texture is wavy, and movement begins with a subtle wave in the hair strands. It can get tangled if not cared for properly. Maintaining control of the frizziness is essential to avoid knotting. I compare this to becoming a preteen and embracing its challenges with guidance. As a pre-teen, there were a lot of changes. I began to do things on my own. I didn't always have a sibling with me. It was exciting but scary to do what I had watched my three older sisters do. When there are many life changes, applying strategies and lessons learned comes in handy.

Curly is the third hair texture, and there are three patterns of curls: Loose, medium, and tight. Teenage and pre-adulthood years are just like those curls. Tricky and unpredictable. Some refer to the fourth coily hair as bad, undesirable hair. This texture has three patterns: coily, tightly coiled, and zig-zag. It is difficult to achieve the desired curls if someone is uncertain about their texture and curl pattern. Like adulthood, the coily hair type requires patience and consistency in figuring out which hair regimen works for you. You may have to switch things up along the way to achieve healthy hair. I had a plan for my life, but nothing went as planned.

I learned to:

- Assess where I am, and choose to make it a starting point
- Be okay with what I have assessed and bring goals into my mind
- Commit to creating goals and a plan of execution.

I am taking my braids out. My older sister Faniesha and I are talking and laughing when suddenly, she stops and says, "What's wrong with your face?" We argue about whether nothing or something is wrong until Faniesha says, "Go look in the mirror!" In the bathroom mirror, I cannot believe what I see. I close my eyes and open them, close, and open them again. I smile and stop smiling. Flare my nostrils out and in. There is no movement on the left side of my face.

I was diagnosed with a severe case of Bell's Palsy at seventeen years old. According to the doctor, it will still look like I had a stroke if I recover. People can recover from this, though there is sometimes minor neurological damage. When we got the news, my mother responded passionately with two words, "BUT GOD." Faith is her foundation.

All I thought about was what it would be like going back to school and getting through my senior year of high school. It made me so nervous. I thought of some clever comebacks to anyone who made fun of me. I can always see when someone notices my face, but I wish people would ask or say something instead of staring. I decided to stop working my summer job at the hospital daycare. I spend time with Ma, and every day she gives me a regimen that includes herbs, teas, and a face massage. And every day, I deal with the emotional pain of seeing my face disfigured.

Ma never gives details of her childhood. I know she was shy and always spoke of how cruel kids can be. I'm guessing she may have been bullied. Regardless, Ma is compassionate, honest, and determined to raise four strong independent black women and two black men. I have love and respect for her. Even when she works full time, Ma makes sure we are well cared for. She is an entrepreneur and artist who can look at anything and recreate it.

All summer, I loved laying in her lap and listening. "People will always have something negative to say about you, whether you are doing great or struggling. Forget about the opinions of others and focus on how you feel about yourself. If you are feeling negative about yourself, which may happen, remember you have the power to change how you feel about yourself." I carried this with me and began to accept myself differently. It felt freeing to notice people's judgment and choose to ignore it. These lessons of self-love grounded me during countless adversities.

By the time I go back to school, the muscles in my face are more relaxed, as if touched by Ma's prayers. Despite the occasional numbness or reversion of one eye closing more than the other, I looked like myself again. I felt new confidence, and I was excited about senior year. I love learning and making the honor roll, but graduating means ending a chapter and beginning a new chapter where I am independent. During the first few weeks, some kids noticed the slight droop on the left side of my face and asked what had happened to me over the summer. They are more curious than cruel. Occasionally, someone makes a joke, but it does not bother me. But Tonya, my best friend, is not having it. Since our nursing class in the ninth grade, we have shared similar class schedules. Tonya has high energy, is outgoing, and is in your face; I am quiet, calm, observant, and warm once you get to know me. Our friendship feels balanced. Tonya always finds me at my locker in the morning, ready to tell me about something that happened the night before. She defended me and felt like she needed to protect my feelings. I appreciate it, but I know how to defend myself. Some kids mistake me for being shy and try to pick on me, but I am tough from years of fighting with my five siblings. I only fought a few times in high school until people realized they should not mess with me even though I am quiet.

I create hairstyles for so many young girls. Addie, for example, is feisty and unafraid to speak her mind. Since she was a little girl, I have been doing her hair and enjoyed watching her grow into her personality. Addie's hair is coily, and it can tangle easily. She doesn't like that. Addie was always feisty as a young girl. At six years old, she would say, "that's hair, you know," because she never liked her hair pulled. Although her hair detangles easily today, we always laugh thinking about how rough it was to comb her hair as a young child. Recently, she asked me to 'fix her sideburns'. She has more hair there than she wants. I coached her through laying her hair down, "put some of the product on your finger. Now draw a C on the temple area and repeat until all hair is smooth and the product is dry".

Addie complains that it isn't working and wants me to cut it. Of course, she needs permission from her mother to cut it, and mom says no. She confided in me about the kids making fun of her hairline. I gave her some words of encouragement my mother gave me--reassuring her that we all have imperfections and that self-love is essential because it easily outweighs people's criticism. 'We are all created differently, and you are perfect the way you are. You have to choose to look in the mirror and embrace what you are. Would you prefer to have no hair on your head?' "No!" 'Even if you don't have hair, you are beautifully and wonderfully made. True beauty reflects from the inside out.' the outer world can create images of beauty, but we can choose what we deem beautiful.

I give patience and care to each person who sits in my chair. Some of my clients deal with scalp issues, alopecia, and thinning hairlines, and helping them reach their hair goals has become one of my favorite things to do as a cosmetologist. Many people come to me because someone they know has referred them. I have one client who knew three of my clients, and each spoke highly of me and reassured her I would be able to help. During her first visit, we just talked for a while about the condition of her hair. Like all first-time clients, I asked open-ended questions to peek into her hair regimen and the desired look. From there, we get to the root of their hair issues, and I give recommendations that promote healthy hair. Some people assume they have 4C hair when they actually have wavy hair that just needs some TLC. The truth is no person's hair is unruly. It's never as bad as they think.

Your lifestyle can affect the condition of your hair. The environment you live in, whether the air is dry or moist, whether the water is hard, your job or life stressors, the foods you eat, and the vitamins you take. Medication and hormonal imbalances can play a role as well. Our blood sends nutrients through our body, including the hair.

When I first met Donna, I was the manager of an extremely busy salon in a mall. She sat patiently waiting her turn as I handled salon issues, informing other clients when they would be serviced and helping a team member with some personal issues. That day was chaotic, but she sat very patiently with a smile on her face. Although I was servicing her, Donna's positive energy lifted me when she came in. From then on, I looked forward to her appointments. Donna has beautiful coily hair, and it shrinks 90%. After a blowout, her hair falls below her shoulders; before, it looked like a two-inch afro. Over the years, I helped her manage minor dry scalp issues and deep cleaned her curls, which grew nicely for her. Donna followed me to where I work now, and one day she revealed that she had cancer and would begin receiving chemotherapy. Donna wanted me to cut her hair. She didn't want to go through the phase of her hair falling out and said it was only fitting for me to cut it because I had cared for her hair for many years. It was an honor to do this for her. She loved her hair and how much it had grown but was willing to let it go.

Her son came with her to the shop. It was early in the morning, so just a few people were in the shop. As you enter the shop, there are 4 stations on the right and 6 to the left. My station was the last one on the left. I always preferred the last station in the shop. I am ready with the clippers and combs at my station. I see her eyes look over at the clippers and quickly turn away. Although she was embracing what was, I could see that it was hard for her. I put the cape on her, and we exchanged casual conversation. I began the consultation to clarify her desired look, and shortly after, I delivered—another happy client.

Months before high school graduation, I was diagnosed with Blount's disease. This bone disorder causes the tibia (shin bone) to angle inward. At times, my right leg buckles, and I fall. My parents took me to many doctors to address my severe bow-leggedness as a child. According to the doctors, I would grow out of it. I did not. For some people, Blount's disease is painless and corrected without surgery. While undiagnosed, degenerative arthritis developed in my right knee, making surgery mandatory.

I decided to wait to have the surgery because I did not want to be walking across the stage on crutches at graduation. I walked across the stage with joy and celebrated with all the seniors at grad night. There were games, face painting, and rooms with activities set up. I was friendly with everyone and had so much fun.

About two weeks later, I had my first surgery, and the doctor placed metal into my bone. I was nervous and curious about being put to sleep and wondered how waking up from the anesthesia would feel. The surgeon cut into my leg to remove a two-inch wedge from my shin and put a rod down the center of the bone to help keep my leg straight. They also turned my right foot outward. Because of the intricate hardware, the doctors did not give me a cast. The rod, plate, and screws held everything together and prevented my bone from overgrowing. I was hospitalized for three days with drainage tubes in my leg. They remove pus, blood, or other fluids from the wound. It grossed me out. The doctor monitored my vital signs and ensured I received proper circulation in my legs.

I can feel my bones shifting on the ride home. I begged for a cast, but the doctor reassured us that the plate and rod made the cast unnecessary. Allowing my bones to fuse into the hardware is a matter of patience.

Although I studied nursing all four years of high school, I knew I wouldn't become a nurse. I earned my certifications and briefly worked in a nursing home, where I spent time with elders who didn't have a family. I would talk, laugh or just sit with them to keep them company for a while. It would make me sometimes cry, hearing them tell stories of loneliness. My summer days are spent in physical therapy sessions and figuring out what adulthood will look like for me come September.

For the first time, I was alone very often. Faniesha was working and taking college courses, and my twin brothers, JJ and Donnell, worked at a clothing store. Recovery was challenging, and I wanted to give up and give in to my pain at first, sleep through the day, and wait for my family to come home. After a while, this got old to me. I felt bored and unproductive. I was not used to being alone, but the quiet time helped me discover myself and regain my strength. I began reading self-help books and thinking about the life I wanted. One day I decided my bedside commode was no longer an option. Birdbaths were no longer an option because it was too hard to manage the shower.

I tried to move more and more every day, even when I was in pain. I began to ignore the pain and focus on my burning desire to overcome it. I crawled and wobbled until one day, I could stand and hop. It took me a year to teach myself to walk again. I learned how to persevere through physical pain. I learned about my power over pain. Pain can be crippling, but I can choose how I think and respond to pain. I listen to my body, but ultimately I define my pain and choose to keep going despite it. I keep moving forward.

Allowing my body to heal was a process that taught me patience as a teenager. I tell my clients to trust the process when working toward their hair goals– whether they are growing their hair, transitioning to natural hair, or healing their scalp. When I first got released from the hospital, I used a walker. As I got stronger, I transitioned to crutches and then a cane. I took tiny steps and found different ways to move until I no longer needed the extra assistance. Sometimes I would feel unstable. I would assess what wasn't working and build my upper body strength. I help my clients determine what isn't working and give them tools to make the appropriate changes to make their hair stronger.

Your blueprint to healthy hair will differ from another person's. Be patient and intentional about your hair care to achieve your hair goals.

# CHAPTER 2

# Tackling Adulthood

The second summer after high school, I took morning courses twice a week at the community college and majored in early childhood development. Math and English are easy, but the computer course is a struggle. I work full-time at the hospital daycare, where I volunteered as a teacher's aide. I worked with a class of fifteen, five, and six-year-old children. Although I was an aide, I was often left to attend to the children alone. They always said they had a job for me when I was ready.

I managed schoolwork and worked two jobs because I was driven and loved keeping myself occupied. I also worked part-time as a parking attendant at Washington Redskins stadium. The daycare was flexible with my schooling and the stadium hours rarely overlapped. Working at the stadium required constant movement, walking, and waving cars along, and the daycare was just as busy.

I realized early on that being around babies made me feel happy. My older sister Sierra had children very young. Her first baby was born when I was nine years old, and I loved caring for all my nieces and nephews as if they were mine. There was an adorable boy at the daycare, and I was the only one who could get him to stop crying every day. There was a big window above the classroom area. Parents could observe the children without disrupting the class. While mom signed him in, I would prepare for him. It took me twenty minutes to calm him down the first few times. I reassured him that mommy would return at the end of the day. When she came to pick him up, I would remind him about our conversation before he clung to her. During the day, he would ask for or find me if anything was wrong. I loved it.

One day I worked aftercare, looking after all children from five to ten years old with the other aides. The children were loud, rowdy, and unresponsive to all my directives. To gain the attention of the larger group, I raised my voice and instructed everyone to return to their seats. The next day, I was called into the administrative office with three staff members. The center director allowed the lead teachers to leave the aides in the classroom alone while they hung out upstairs after lunch. Parents filed a verbal abuse accusation, and we were all fired. I was angry about everything. I was making good money ($13 an hour) plus my time working at the stadium. Both positions allowed me to get what I needed for school and give my parents money toward the bills and household necessities. I knew I would miss working there. I had become closer with my co-worker Gena because we rode the same bus to and from work. We lived about five minutes from each other and always discussed the happenings at work. She lost her job that day too. Gena and her family sued and won their lawsuit against them. I was eligible for unemployment and decided to apply for unemployment to cover my financial responsibilities.

I woke up early and dressed in a white button-down shirt and a pink floral skirt with sandals. I wanted to look professional but also stay cool in the heat. When I arrived, the office was packed. After about two hours of standing in line and asking question after question and answering questions, I was able to submit all the necessary paperwork.

My childhood friend DJ said he would give me a ride so I would not have to walk home in the heat. He took too long. I was tired of waiting and decided to walk across the parking lot to the bus stop. DJ was the friend I turned to when I wanted to escape from my world of responsibility. He knew things about me that nobody else did. DJ was a very handsome boy. He wasn't very tall, but he had just the right height for me. With his medium build and broad shoulders, I always looked forward to seeing him. He kept a fresh haircut and always smelled so nice. Outside of my family, I always stayed to myself. I liked to sit out on the porch, and his best friend lived next door to me. Whenever he came over, I spoke to him politely but never paid him any mind. Eventually, he asked for my number, and I gave it to him because I felt so comfortable talking to him. We started hanging out when we were sixteen and became closer. There was unavoidable energy exchanged whenever we were together. There was no judgment, and I valued our friendship. We hung out in the neighborhood but didn't go too many places together. I lost my virginity to him, and we wanted to keep our intimate friendship private.

Parents always say *stranger danger*, but they never say a familiar face can be dangerous too. A car drives past and slows down. He put his car in reverse and asked, "Do you want a ride?"

The man who offered me a ride worked at the hospital. As a volunteer, I would deliver paperwork to a different floor, and he would appear. When I ate lunch in the cafeteria, he was there too. Everywhere I went, I would see him. Unfortunately, at fifteen years old, I did not pay attention or think much of things like this. After I started working part-time, I would see him from time to time because the daycare was also in the hospital. He would offer me a ride, but I never had the need. It is so hot that stepping outside means breaking a sweat, so I welcome a ride to get out of the heat. When I get in the car, he says he is in the process of moving and asks if he can pick up a box from his house first. I say okay, and we pull up to his apartment right across the street. His car does not have air conditioning, and he doesn't want me to be hot while he gathers his stuff, so we walk into the building and up the stairs to the apartment.

I see dozens of boxes and things and a couch in the center of the room. He tells me I can sit and that he will be right back. I hear him moving around in the back room and his footsteps coming back toward the living room. When I look up, there he is, dashing toward me. It all happens so quickly. He is on top of me, forcing my skirt up. When I start fighting him, he pulls a knife and puts it on my neck. "Don't move." I tense up, so terrified I do not know what to do. He wrestles with me, then presses the knife harder against my neck. "Relax, and I will let you leave." While I cry, he proceeds, finishes, and gets up. Don't move". As I lay there, he walked to the back room. I moved and ran home.

Ma is there. She says, "How was your day? How did everything go?" All I could get out was, "Good."

Nothing feels worse. Life has ended, and I believe it is my fault. If I never got in the car. If I wore something different. If I didn't talk to him and if I wasn't so friendly to him at the hospital, maybe...

I kept it all to myself for a few months, hoping to move on and forget about it all. I received $300 monthly for unemployment and was able to pick up more hours as a parking attendant. One night I had to walk from the entrance to the back of the lot, which was the distance of half of a football field. I felt tired and had to sit because my breathing became so heavy. This shortness of breath continued for two weeks. I say to myself, *Girl, you need to lose some weight. You can't even walk from one side to the other.*

One night, after a shower, I took my towel off to put lotion on and my underclothes. I shared a room with my sister Faniesha, who sat on her bed. "Do you have something to tell me"?

I knew my stomach had gotten a little bigger, but I've always been a juicy girl, so I figured I was gaining weight. But Faniesha knew my body, so the question held my attention. I went to the store and purchased a three-pack of pregnancy tests. While I walked, my mind was racing.

*I can't be pregnant. I haven't had sex in months. I can't be pregnant. I'm still getting my monthly cycle. I can't be pregnant. I'm only 19, well, 20 in a few weeks.* My heartbeat was fast while I opened the packaging and read the instructions. I prepared to wait a few minutes and put the cap back on the first test. Two lines appeared fast. *No waiting? This one must be broken.* I quickly repeated the steps, and two lines appeared, faster than the last. *Oh no, I can't be! This third one will show me.* Again, there are two lines. I took the test into the room for Faniesha to see. "What are you going to do?". 'I don't know...I need help'.

We called my oldest sister Theresa, and she agreed to take me to get a blood test for confirmation. I laid in bed that night, unable to sleep at all. I felt like a failure, afraid, confused, and unsure of what would happen next. I had not lived up to my parent's expectations and was contemplating the feeling of failing them. *How am I going to have a baby? I feel like I'm still just a child myself. I was just starting to get into the rhythm of being an adult.*

The following day, Theresa came to pick me up, and we went to three different clinics: the first one was closed, and the next one was too busy to see me. Due to a slight complication, I took a urine test instead of a blood test at the third clinic. Positive again. The date of conception was indeed the same day as the sexual assault. Theresa encouraged me to tell our parents, but she would help as best she could if I chose not to.

## CHAPTER 3

# Faith and Family

This Sunday, my family is getting ready for church. Everyone is showered, dressed, and eating breakfast. My parents are still upstairs getting dressed. They always take their showers last. Our two-story, three-bedroom, one-bathroom house had just enough space for us. My twin brothers share a room, and Faniesha and I share a room. When Theresa and Sierra lived in the house, they had one room, and as the younger siblings, the four of us shared a room. I remember taking turns getting dressed, but sharing with my brother was easy. We all were used to it. Although I sometimes wished for my own room, I loved how that small space made us function as a team and fostered unconditional love.

Since moving out, Theresa has been working and building her family. She was a teacher for a few years and even worked at the zoo. That's where she met her husband. Sometimes we would spend the night with them. Their first place was a one-bedroom apartment, and we all made the best of our time there. Staying in her apartment was like staying at Big Granma's house. We made the small space work by putting sheets and blankets on the floor to get comfortable while we slept there for the weekends.

Theresa loves cooking and hosting family gatherings so she can cook. When she and her family moved into a three-bedroom house, the extra space made her place extra fun. It was just like being at home, never alone, with someone constantly invading your space. There is never a dull moment. Someone is always doing something, whether it's a fight between the kids or somebody getting in trouble for some silly thing they did. We would play games and dress up using random objects around the house. Sometimes we would all watch TV. Theresa's husband loved watching *Star Trek* and would shush us if we talked too much. Faneisha would get so mad.

My sister Sierra was consistently in and out of our lives. As a child, Sierra would sneak out of the house and sneak people into the house. Ma and Daddy worked a lot, so Sierra often babysat us. One time she wanted to have her friends over and watch music videos. Of course, Sierra couldn't have her four younger siblings in the house, so what did Sierra do? She locked us in the room and said we better not tell or else. Well, Faniesha was not having it, threatened or not; Faniesha was still going to tell. Sierra gave us some snacks and said she would be back after her friends left. The four of us watched TV, and when we got bored, we would make up hand games. My favorite hand game was Slaps, where one person's palm goes on top of the other. The person whose palm is on the bottom must try to hit their partner's backhand. We played so well together it was easy to be stuck in a room together.

Even though Sierra wasn't outright neglectful, Faniesha still didn't like it, and she snitched on her anyway. It's called dry snitching. Sierra got punished, and she couldn't talk on the phone for a week, which was hard because she loved talking on the phone to her friends. Later, Sierra hit Faniesha for getting her in trouble. Since then, there has always been this unspoken tension between them.

Sierra would pick me up from Aunt Debbie's house after school when I was in kindergarten. One day I didn't get picked up. She had run away from home. Sierra's skin is much lighter than all of us, my parents included. She favors my mom, but her skin is just a little lighter. People would always say that she didn't look like us. Growing up, my aunt always separated us from her. Although she is our biological aunt, our bond is weak. Sierra's teenage years were troubling, and she began using drugs. Sierra was involved with the family, but she might disappear for a while if she disagreed with my mom.

When mom and dad were working and Theresa was out, Faniesha had to step in and help with Sierra's children. She let her feelings be known--*whoever gave birth to the baby should be the one taking care of the baby.* I understood Faniesha's point, but I cherished helping take care of my nieces and nephews. At this point, Sierra has four children. Three of her children live with Theresa, and our parents have custody of Sierra's baby girl. I cared for her a lot because I was in the house more after losing my job at the hospital daycare.

Me, Faniesha, Donnell, and J.J do almost everything together. We study the Bible, play board games, and wrestle with each other. My mom would join in; it was always boys against the girls. We would pick our opponent. We all line up in the tiny family room, looking into each other's eyes, trying to keep a serious face, but cracking a smile. My dad never wrestled, but he would start us up by pushing us into the other. We'd reenact a scene from WWE, fake punches, staged body slams, artificial elbows to the back, or ribs. All of this with the sounds of laughter bouncing off the walls.

Although Theresa and Sierra had it a little different than the four of us, we were a unit. Not only did we play together, but we would also get punished together too. If any of us did something wrong, we would all get in trouble together. Theresa and Sierra were allowed to hang out with friends and go to the mall and movies, get jobs, and have boyfriends at a young age. That was not the case for us, not because we were bad children, but because Theresa and Sierra were typical teenagers who took advantage of their freedom, which made my parents stricter.

As the four of us grew closer, we became creative with owning our freedom. As teenagers, we all went to school, work, and home, and made the honor roll, played instruments, and sang in the choir. All the activities made it easy for us to disappear sometimes and have fun with our friends. We all respected our parents, so we were careful if we broke the rules. No one would have guessed I was having sex at sixteen or skipping school now and then.

I always put pressure on myself because I never wanted to disappoint them. I held myself to the standard my parents taught me and strived for perfection. When I fell short, I felt inadequate. Today was one of those days. I was hard on myself for being irresponsible and reckless at times. I thought that they would never see me as their baby girl again once I told them.

My parents come downstairs, and we all get into the van on this day. Off we go on what feels like the longest ride ever. Usually, our car rides are filled with talking and laughter. Today Faniesha, Donnell, and JJ are chatting as usual, but I have so much on my mind I don't even feel like talking to pass the time. Soon I would have to tell my parents about my pregnancy and the assault.

We have always been a faith-based family, even if we did not attend church every Sunday. I grew up going to a small church in Washington, D.C. When my family joined a new church, I was seventeen. A sweet woman named Val counseled me, and she told me if I ever needed anything she would always be there. My parents are in the choir, so we sit with our friends during the service. Praise and worship are what I enjoy most about church services. Music feeds my soul. My family quickly became involved with church members. Having well-known and active parents in the church is hard because church members hold you to an unreasonable standard.

I enjoyed the small church setting, but the congregation was growing quickly. The church now has its building, and they have expanded into a school, but back then, Sunday services were at a local high school, which was very different. The school was huge, and certain areas and classrooms were for Sunday school. A few times, in the beginning, I just sat outside and enjoyed the air because I couldn't find my way. After about a month, I had it down. A long hallway at the entrance leads to the stairs, and the seating area is in the large auditorium two flights down.

During today's service, I didn't hear the pastor at all. I was contemplating how to tell my parents. When the music and invitation for prayer began, I regained my hearing. "If your heart is heavy, and you need prayer, come. Don't worry about the person next to you...just come". I tapped Faniesha and moved toward the aisle. Faniesha knows what I'm about to do, and she grabs my hand. "Do you want me to go with you"? I decided to do this on my own.

When I went up to pray and seek guidance, there Val was. Her expression and demeanor were comforting, but it was hard to look her in the eyes and tell her I was pregnant.

"It will be okay. I'm with you all the way," was her response. I tell her it is all a mistake. "Nothing happens by accident. Everything has a purpose. Your baby is no accident". After she gave more words of love, encouragement, reassurance, and prayer, Val told me I needed to talk with my parents, and she came with me. Val was really with me all the way. When we got outside, many people were standing and talking as usual. I was wondering where we should talk. There are several benches along the walkway toward the front of the building. It was a large open space that allowed many people to gather at one time. Val and I sat on the last bench to the left, which took me away from the crowd and gave us personal space to have a conversation. Ma was sitting down, and dad was standing beside her. They told Donnell, JJ, and Faniesha to go to the van while we talked.

I told them I had something very important to say but almost couldn't get it out because I cried so hard. I could hear the chatter of others around us and was surprised at the concern people had, but Val steered people away, protecting me and my secret.

Ma started crying with me and said, "Whatever it is, we will figure it out." I took a deep breath, and the words just flowed out. I told my parents about the sexual assault and the pregnancy. It was the hardest thing I'd ever had to do. I have a respectful fear of my parents, but I see Daddy as a force field not to be played with. I was most anxious about his response. He hugs me with tears in his eyes and says, "Babygirl, we will get through this." At that moment, I felt calm energy take over me. Although I felt like an epic failure, my dad made me feel secure and supported. Ma asked many questions, and I hated thinking back and saying everything. I waited to tell them I had been sexually active beforehand. I could have died.

When we got home, we had a family meeting. Family meetings are like business meetings. Dad leads the conversation, beginning with how proud he is and pointing out individual accomplishments before reminding us of his expectations. We respected one another, never cut each other off, and listened carefully to each other. It was a space to be unafraid to speak our truths. During this meeting, I was the topic of discussion, and my siblings showered me with love. They each supported me in different ways. Faniesha was incredibly supportive, giving words of love and encouragement. She has always been protective of me. Faniesha said, 'MY BABY' when I arrived home from the hospital. Despite any epic arguments or disagreements, our love keeps us tight. I never spoke directly to the twins about it. Dad talked with them and explained that he wanted them to make sure they supported me as much as possible.

I told Sierra one day when she came to visit, days after I told my parents. She was angry with me for not telling her sooner. Sierra said no matter where she was or what she was doing, she would come and help me if anything happened again. During our conversation, I learned that it happened to her as well. She met a guy and trusted him, but he enjoyed assaulting her, and that's how she got pregnant with her second baby. One day, he left her in the house, and she decided to run. After a few months at home, she realized she was pregnant. She walked around for months pretending just to be gaining weight. Sierra decided not to tell anyone because she felt it didn't matter. No one would believe her because everyone was used to her lying. I believed her.

My parents took me to the police station to file a report the next day. I was frustrated during my interview because the officer posed questions as if I was lying. The added stress could hurt me, and the baby and my parents did not want him to know about the pregnancy. After speaking with a lawyer, my father learned that the description was similar to a few other sexual assault reports. He talked to a lawyer and followed the case, but I stayed uninvolved. The man who sexually assaulted me was convicted and sentenced to 20 years to life in prison with the evidence in the collective cases against him.

CHAPTER 4

# Emotional Triggers and Counseling

I was not myself. Between July and November, I was irritable, distrustful, and opposed to meeting new people, especially men. I was misplacing the hurt and anger that stemmed from the sexual assault for quite some time. My thoughts, moods, and behaviors had changed, and I couldn't always understand why. Sometimes I wanted nothing to do with men, and other times I longed for revenge. Men find me attractive, and some even say I am cute for a thick girl. This statement is triggering. I decided I was going to get them before they got me. I took full advantage of men and lured money or things I did not need, just for the satisfaction of taking from men. I was sure to leave them as wounded as I felt. At the time, I did not understand how much damage I was causing to men who truly wanted to get to know me.

My body responded to the physical and emotional pain. The physical pain subsided after a few weeks, yet emotional pain is ever-present for years after. Triggers come in various forms, and the nervous system becomes more sensitive with each trigger. An outside source activates triggers. For me, it was people's behavior or comments that triggered within me a fear of abandonment, especially within friendships. I did not want to be left again without communication. I tended to withdraw when I felt triggered or misunderstood. Identifying triggers and understanding where they stem from helps process trauma and change behavioral responses.

Mrs. Pittman was my first cosmetology mentor. She said everyone in the industry has a thing they do the best naturally. I move through textured hair with no problem, and because of her guidance, I specialize in natural hair care. Mrs. Pittman taught me many things about hair care and tricks of the trade. I listened and valued her words because I knew I could speak freely. She never judged me; she just offered me guidance and challenged me to see different perspectives. One day, Mrs. Pittman asked if I had a boyfriend. I replied, "I don't want a boy for a friend." She laughed and asked me who hurt me. After I opened up to her, she said, "Hurt people hurt people." At that moment, the statement penetrated me, and I began to self-assess. Mrs. Pittman encouraged me to get counseling. I got the feeling she may have had a similar experience.

I can remember me talking stuff out in my head. *Get it together. You don't have time to be emotional. You got to get it together.* What I processed internally gave me awareness regardless of the emotional upset. Functioning from a place of pain only leads to more pain. More pain for yourself and the others involved. I believe emotional pain is the worst type because it's like living in anger and bitterness and unaware of why. When I considered the possibility of inflicting emotional pain, I became committed to doing the work to heal. I kept so many things to myself, and it took me some time to follow through with finding a counselor.

I began attending group counseling sessions at a crisis pregnancy center my parents found twice a week. I talked with the therapist and two girls. Keisha was eighteen and living in a shelter. Her parents kicked her out of the house for getting pregnant, and her child's father was not around. Nikki was only sixteen. Her child's father wanted to keep their baby with his family. Nikki's mom hoped counseling would help her rethink giving up her child so easily.

I continued working at the stadium until my supervisor told me to consider switching positions or resigning. It was clear that walking through the lots was way too much for me, whether I wanted to admit it or not. Listening to these girls share their lives, I remained thankful for having so much love and support from my family. I was not hoping to gain anything from the sessions but was open to it because my parents felt it would be good for me.

I learned more about my body and how a woman becomes pregnant during therapy. I had been sexually active the same week of the sexual assault. After class, he picked me up, and I went to his house. We talked for a while, and then we had sex. The doctor confirmed the date of conception, so I never questioned my pregnancy, but doubt set in after learning how long sperm stays inside the body.

I was unsure if my pregnancy resulted from sex with DJ or the sexual assault. Again, I turned to Theresa, who advised me to talk to him. I was very nervous about calling him but also optimistic about his reaction. When I told him, DJ explained he couldn't have a child because he would get kicked out of his mother's house.

Then he started saying disrespectful and spiteful comments about all the guys he saw coming in and out of my house, knowing how big my family is, but every guy was there to see me. *I thought he was my friend. I thought he knew me. So many people live in my house. He assumed that every guy who came to my door was coming to see me. I wish he were able to tell me how he really feels. I know he is scared, but how does he think I feel?* I thought all that to myself because I didn't feel like giving him any extra energy. I never got the chance to tell him that a man assaulted me that day; he was late picking me up. I hung up. I needed to focus on myself.

DJ became a ghost. Not only did I lose a good friend, but DJ also snatched my chance to find out if the twins were from him or the sexual assault. I didn't know who my children's father was and was unsure if I would ever find out. I decided not to tell my parents about him. I didn't want to put more on my family, and I felt it was enough emotional stress on my parents. Only my sisters knew I was uncertain about my child's father.

Counseling became an annoyance. I wanted to figure things out on my own, and the therapist was pushy. She constantly asked leading questions about how I might feel after seeing my baby for the first time. She asked questions about it every session. Maybe she thought she was helpful or learned this in school, but in reality, she was planting a thought I never considered. She spoke as if she knew I would hate my child. I would usually sit, listen and give her minimal responses. I just could not fathom hating my baby at first sight. One day I decided it was my last session. I could no longer tolerate her Negative Nancy attitude.

"So you're telling me I will hate my child because of how they were conceived? I haven't even expressed any negative feelings to you, but you think you're helping by introducing me to all these negative feelings?!" The therapist was quiet for a while and then asked how I felt about my pregnancy for the first time. "Don't you think you should have asked me this from the beginning?" I walked out and told my parents that it was the last session. They accepted that without question. In some ways, I learned to manage pain on my own. Ma and Daddy always checked in with me and made space to express my emotions, but I didn't always share. The most consistent question was, are you okay? Even if things weren't OK at the moment, I believed they would be, so I always said, I'm okay.

My parents highly respect our pastor and suggested he counsel me. I was open to it, but I anticipated he would quote a lot of scripture and talk to me about sin. Speaking with Pastor was nothing like I imagined. His voice was smooth and comforting. "Hello. What brings you to see me?" I told him about my pregnancy and the sexual assault. And about DJ. His face never changed. I expected to see judgment in his expression, but it never came. There was empathy in his eyes as I told my story. The most important thing he said to me was, "This is your life, and you must make choices for yourself." He did give me scriptures to read. Seek God and do not lean on my understanding. Trust in the word of God. We had a few more sessions which went pretty much the same way. He listened and never formed an opinion but gave me scripture to read.

After one of our sessions, he recommended I speak to a church member named Beverly. When I first started talking to her, it was only in passing. I would stop by her office occasionally and casually talk about things going on in my life, and she listened. She validated my thoughts and asked questions that challenged me to think differently. I'd stop in for clarity, create a plan of action and then disappear for months or years at a time. I was navigating myself through obstacles by understanding where I was and envisioning where I wanted to be. I would then create a game plan and move toward the execution. I understood the demands of motherhood and mapped out how I'd get there. *I'll learn to be a mom for a year and then figure out school and work.*

I often turned to Val for guidance, although she was a professional photographer and not a counselor. She was in a prayer group and remains someone I can always turn to. God puts specific people in your path to speak to you. We all receive messages differently. Sometimes it is difficult to receive a message depending on who gives it and how it is given. But then there are those specific people WE HEAR when they speak.

Outside of Beverly, I was referred to counselors, and most visits gave me a headache. It felt like no one understood me. I would sit in a session, and before it was over, I decided it was my first and last session. If a counselor had given personal input on my life, I would not return. I have benefited from counselors who listened and gave me tools to think and navigate life positively and productively. Some counselors are unable to understand their patient's needs fully. Finding a counselor is like finding a pair of shoes; they have to be the right fit.

A knot happens when two strands of hair wrap around each other and become intertwined. Once a few more strands intertwine, the knot can become bigger and harder to remove. It can grow bigger when left untreated or unaddressed, causing more obstacles. I compare this to emotional and physical pain. Emotional pain signals the same brain region as physical pain, which suggests that the two are inextricably linked. Emotional pain can cause physical pain. Stress causes muscles and nerves to constrict, causing physical pain and signals to the brain. Trauma resurfaces sooner or later. Emotions can influence the decisions you make in life, big or small. We can choose to hold or release. Trauma causes measurable changes to our DNA and can be inherited like blood type or eye color. As I process trauma, I choose to release trauma as I process it because I do not want my children to endure the same trauma. If you know someone who has lived through sexual assault, be someone they can count on to listen if you can.

Healing from trauma does not happen overnight; it takes time and consistent self-work and self-development. It is best to address the pain directly to begin the healing process. I encourage survivors to talk or write about it as a release. Otherwise, you may carry sorrow and bitterness without processing these emotions. Our emotions are extensions of us, but they are not who we are, and we do not have to act on them. Like a knot, we can acknowledge them, find the root, and gently begin unraveling to heal.

If you are a survivor like me, you may find it difficult to trust or confide in people. At some point, choose to take a leap of faith. Try to confide in people who have shown love and support. Maybe they have helped you in the past. Although it may seem like parents or confidants will not understand, telling them offers them the opportunity to help. Sometimes it takes going to a church or community center. Everyone copes differently with situations they face. When seeking professional counsel, research the counselor/agency providing services. Visit counselors until you are comfortable with one that supports, challenges, and gets you thinking. Give them a few sessions and see how it is working for you. You must be transparent about what you feel, think, and desire for your life. If you don't feel comfortable, that may not be the place of healing for you. Learn what works for you. Seek and find people who are passionate about helping others. The possibilities are endless. The International Association for Counseling (IAC), American Counseling Association (ACA), and sexual assault hotline (RAINN) are available resources. The person who will listen might be your hairstylist.

My sister Teresa is a pastor now. Recently, she invited me to speak at a women's retreat. The first time I publicly spoke about the trauma I experienced, it was more like a testimony. I was excited about this second opportunity to speak, but I didn't know what to say this time. The retreat was titled *Anchored Women* in April, which is recognized nationally as sexual assault awareness month. I sat still, asking God to guide my words, and it came to me. I came along as a supporter and survivor identifying and normalizing reactions and obstacles women face after sexual assault. I encouraged them to voice their feelings and emotions. *Nothing happens by accident. Everything has a purpose.* This statement hits much differently now and has grounded me through countless life hurdles. We cannot conform to the standards, expectations, and beliefs that other people have for us.

# CHAPTER 5

# The Twins

When I found out I was pregnant, I was three months along. There were many doctor's appointments, and I hated all the poking and prodding, but my baby looked healthy after the first two sonograms. Midway through my second trimester, my parents came for my check-up, but I decided to get the sonogram alone. The tech listened for the heartbeat, and I was relieved at the sound. The pictures take longer than usual, though. She pauses and clicks back again and again. "You just have one baby, right?" I wonder what she could see to ask that question, but I try to respond calmly, "of course, why?" She added more gel to the probe and continued to move it around my stomach. To the left, she went. Back to the right then, to the very bottom–she pushes harder. Rolling the probe around, the technician looked confused but tried to keep her face straight. Those few minutes felt like an eternity, and then she said, "I see two heads. I see two heads. I see two heads!" *Two heads?! I am terrified of imagining a two-headed baby. How do you take care of a two-headed baby? Will they have to get separated, or can they even be separated?* All of this swirled through my head as the technician took more pictures. With tears in my eyes, I said, "Ma'am, please say something else. "Honey, you are having twins."

As I left the exam room, so many emotions came with me. A moment of relief and excitement turned into anxiety again. I was relieved to have two healthy heartbeats but unsure how to mother two children at twenty years old without a job. One baby is expensive, but two? I was happy but worried and afraid, but thankful to have my parents in the waiting room. I said, "Guess what." "You're having twins!" Ma says. Big Granma always said I would have twins. The women in my family have a very keen intuition.

Ma gave loving advice and an honest perspective on carrying twins throughout my pregnancy. Having experienced twin pregnancy, my mom knew a lot about what I should and shouldn't do. I wasn't allowed to eat anything spicy and had to keep my feet propped up as often as possible to keep the swelling down. Ma stayed on top of me about eating correctly and taking vitamins. She had a complicated pregnancy with JJ and Donnell, so I always listened to her and other seasoned mothers who shared advice. I rested, ate well, and changed my lifestyle because I wanted healthy babies. Walking helps during pregnancy, but because my baby boy was practically waiting to come into the world, I kept having premature labor pain, so I was instructed not to walk too much.

I decided I wanted to know the sex of the babies and was thrilled when I found out I was having a boy and a girl. Now that I knew I had two, I could feel them in my womb differently. My baby girl took over and pushed my baby boy to the bottom of my womb. He was so low that it caused premature labor. The first time it happened, I didn't know what was happening. My stomach tightened, and I could feel pain moving throughout my body. I panicked, and Ma quickly got me to the emergency room. When doctors saw the position of my baby boy, they gave me medication to stop premature labor and steroids to help the baby's lungs in case they could not stop the contractions. I took several trips back to the emergency room with premature contractions throughout my third trimester. I was so afraid of having them too early or something going wrong.

Weeks into my third trimester, I was irritated by the extra poking and prodding at each doctor's visit. It usually takes a while because the tech has to look at both babies. There was something different about how the tech moved the probe this visit. She was clicking and typing much more than usual. At a certain point, she stopped the exam and left the room. She brought the doctor back in with her, and he said, "It's time for the babies to come." I immediately felt nauseous and tried not to panic. *Two weeks early. After this visit, I was supposed to go shopping and get all necessities: car seats, strollers, bottles, and diapers. What will I have for them now?* The doctor turns to my mother and says, "She needs to rest."

Ma gave me soup, which calmed my stomach. In preparation for induction, I followed every instruction--put my feet up and minimized my movement until 6 am the following day. I didn't fully understand why they needed to induce labor, but Ma had told me it often happens with twins.

As I lay in my bed, my mind was moving. *I'm giving birth tomorrow, and you ain't got no clothes yet. Look at what kind of mom you are starting to be. Ugh, stop being so hard on yourself. It will be ok…But my babies don't have any clothes. Ma and Daddy will help me. They always come through for me. I don't want to be that kind of mom relying on my parents to do everything for my children. What if I can't handle my responsibilities? Breathe, Jerre; you're not going to be that kind of mom.* I tried to imagine what it would be like to push two babies out. I wondered what joys having children would bring.

I arrive at the hospital, and my stomach is in knots. "Babygirl, you're going to be okay. We are with you", Daddy says. Ma fills out most of the paperwork, and once she's finished, I walk into a room with a bed and monitors surrounding it. Something is hanging from the ceiling that looks like a harness. (Little did I know, I would have to put my legs in it later that day.) After I am in the hospital gown, I lay in bed for a moment before getting hooked up to all the monitors. There is a monitor for everything. Monitors for all 3 of our heartbeats. Monitors for the contractions and fetal movements. I get Pitocin, a medication that induces labor and helps to start contractions. So many things stuck to me.

Oh, the pain! I cannot get the epidural until I am five centimeters dilated. The pain feels like a dull knife is scraping across my stomach. The time comes, and the epidural needle hurts so bad, but there is a relief. After that, I am asleep, and I feel my stomach tighten. My labor has become a waiting game. My dad is helping me relax. I am so happy he is in the room, but he made it clear he is leaving the room when I start pushing. I didn't want him to stay anyway. How awkward would that be--my dad seeing all of my everything? Nope. Not okay.

When it was time to push, the doctor and many nurses gathered around me and put my legs in that weird-looking contraption on the ceiling. The doctor tells me to push when they say so and when I feel contractions push hard. My stomach is tightening. The nurse says, "now get ready, push as hard as you can." I was preparing myself, but my body was doing other things. Suddenly, the monitors start going off. Baby B's (my baby girl) heart rate dropped. "Stop pushing...Don't push even if you have the desire to". The monitors are quiet, and Baby B is stable. "Ok, we can start pushing again. Breathe". "No, wait...." The monitors are going crazy. "Her heart rate is dropping fast. We have to move", the doctor says.

I'm so scared. I don't understand what is happening around me. My mom looks afraid, but she stays calm. "Everything is going to be okay." The doctor tells me I can't push the twins out because my baby girl's heart rate won't stabilize. When I push, her heart rate and oxygen levels drop. They rushed me to the operating room. I'm nervous, but my mom gets prepped for the operating room and comes with me. I'm lying completely flat, and mom sits next to my head, calming me and helping me focus. The procedure begins, and I feel the pressure of being opened up. I look up at the stainless steel above my head, and now I can see what they are doing too.

"Baby A is out." I don't hear him cry. While I see and feel them reaching to pull out my baby girl, the monitors go off again. "I can't breathe," I say to my mom. "Stay calm. Everything is going to be ok." They give me oxygen, but I'm still gagging. All I see is black.

I hear my dad's voice. "Babygirl, wake up. Wake up so you can hold your babies." I open my eyes to two babies lying side by side. "Those are not my babies... Why are they so light?" My dad laughs a hearty laugh from a healthy place and says, "Girl, those are our babies." The nurse places them in my arms. I'm feeling so warm inside. After everything, my babies are healthy and strong, over five pounds—the most rewarding moment.

Later, I learned that my baby girl's umbilical cord was wrapped around her neck twice, which caused fetal distress. After the blissful feeling of holding my beautiful babies, I started remembering all I didn't have for them.

My parents came to my room the following day, and I was happy to see them. We talked about the babies' needs, and I expressed my worries about not having a job and the income to provide for them. My dad always told me he would help, but it was hard for me to let them take care of my responsibility. My twins belong to me. I felt like I wasn't a real parent if my parents provided all their needs.

They were reassuring, and we talked for a few hours before the nurses brought my babies to the room. All I wanted to do was hold them and for them to stay in my room overnight. The nurse focused on helping me breastfeed and showed me how to have them both latch on simultaneously. Having two babies to feed every two hours was painful. I tried my best, but my son was very greedy. HE FELT LIKE A VACUUM. I didn't know you could get a scab in certain areas.

My mom and dad returned to the hospital with a few church members. They brought so many clothes for my babies. I was in awe of what I saw. I hadn't known most of these people for very long, but my babies had car seats, t-shirts, socks, and so much more because of them. My dad hugged me and whispered, "I told you not to worry." It's true. God will supply all of your needs when you have faith and believe without a shadow of a doubt. Give thanks for all he has done for you. God gives gifts in challenging situations. I am blessed with two healthy babies.

I was so excited to start my new life as a mother. My nurse came in and asked so many questions and answered all my questions. She wanted to make sure I had everything I needed. I was surprised how much hospitals provided: diapers, wipes, bottles, and many informational resources. Of course, they gave small amounts, but I couldn't be more grateful for every single thing I received. All I could do was look at my babies and say thank you on the ride.

My parents stopped by the church because the ministers wanted to meet the twins before we took them home. We pulled up to the side of the old church building we outgrew. The church had two entrances. We entered from the parking lot toward the long hallway that leads down to the sanctuary. As you walk down, there is one classroom to the left and another to the right. We pass the classroom on the left through the short hallway that leads to the basement stairs. Everything happens there, except Sunday services. All the small groups and church meetings were held there. Bible study was packed at times with standing room only. Church members could have social gatherings in the open space in the basement.

Daddy parks and starts taking the babies out. He refused to let me help. The twins are all bundled up because it is still cold outside. Their car seat covers are pink and blue, and our favorite deacon helps Daddy open the seat covers to reveal their tiny bodies and pale skin. We walk inside, and Deacon Wingfield is so excited to see the twins and takes their first picture. "Come on, let's go downstairs." The hallway was very quiet, and the overhead lights were low. As I enter, the lights come on. SURPRISE!!! I was shocked to see a room full of family and friends. I saw the joy on my sister's and brother's faces and my heartfelt warmth. I turned to look at my dad, "I told you, Babygirl." At that moment, I gained a proper understanding of blind faith, believing in something even though you can't see it.

There was a giant blue and pink cake with the cutest baby figurines and so many different types of food. Everyone wanted a chance to hold the twins and take pictures. My favorite picture is of the twins and me with their godparents. The excitement and love on their faces were so precious. My dad had explained that if anything happened to me, my children's godparents would raise them. I had thought hard about who would love and care for my children the same way I would. My mom helped me think deeper about my choice and told me to consider the value of friendships, which were few and far between because of my strong distrust of people. There were few people I could depend on.

During my pregnancy, I spent a lot of time at T's house visiting her mom, who has always been a tremendous source of support, encouragement, and motivation. I trust T with my life and the lives of my twins. I am grateful that she carries them in her heart as I do without question. T was a huge help when I was getting through cosmetology school and has done so much to support me in achieving my goals.

The day I brought my twins home was the day of their baby shower. I opened gifts wearing a plate on my head with a pink bow. I received bibs, bottles, wipes, milk, diapers, clothes, shoes, and more. The gifts lasted until the twins were two years old. Everything I need and more is gifted to me at my surprise baby shower. My twins are so loved. As the evening was winding down, Big Granma said to me, "Nothing but God."

Dry hair can creep up on you like fear. When hair is not getting or retaining enough moisture, dry hair develops. Recognizing the condition of the hair or the state of the fear presents an opportunity to make a change. Dry hair can limit your hair growth, just like fear can stunt your personal growth and development in life.

Oily or greasy hair is comparable to the opinions of others. The oil is beneficial, or it's a problem, depending on the hair type. It is essential to recognize when an opinion is valid; opinions can be helpful or simply a hindrance that is best to ignore completely.

My first night with the twins was an introduction to my new world. I couldn't sleep because the babies were in bed with me, and I was afraid that I would move wrong and roll over on them. Fatboy cried first that night. This was my indication just to feed both of them. I sat on the side of my bed and scooped Fatboy into my arms, securing him in one arm, then scooping Ladybug into my other arm, holding them tightly. I made my way down the stairs to the kitchen. My brother Donnell was the first to appear because the twins began to cry while I made their bottles.

I wasn't moving fast enough. I began to sleep downstairs on the sofa, and the twins slept in the crib my parents set up for me in the living room. I felt better about these sleeping arrangements. Although our house didn't have much space, my parents would figure out how to accommodate all of us. Every once in a while, I would sleep upstairs, and my sister would stay downstairs with the twins. This was helpful because sometimes they didn't want to sleep, and I would be exhausted. Two crying babies became easier with support from my family. There were times when I couldn't get the bottle ready fast enough, and Fatboy cried so hard at times. Ladybug would sit patiently while he fed first. Oh, but the times when she wanted to eat first were challenging. My brothers were so eager to help. They would get up at night with me to help feed and change the twins. I loved learning to be a mom.

After having the twins, I joined the young mom's ministry. Women from my church would visit and bring me diapers and other essentials. Sometimes I would get cases of milk too. Mrs. P was a significant factor because she would bring a care package with all a baby may need, from wipes to socks and t-shirts.

As a new young mother, people always gave their opinions on my life. I didn't listen most times. Depending on the person, I'd only take some of what they said. My dad would say, "chew the meat and spit out the bones but always listen." A lady asked me to consider adopting the twins while I was pregnant. She was in the choir with my parents, so she knew the details of what had happened to me. I couldn't believe she had the nerve to come to me when I didn't ask for her advice. I told her I wanted to have them and raise them myself. She continued to ask me periodically if I considered her offer. How rude was that?

Despite the circumstances, my children have everything they need. I sometimes felt angry with myself for getting pregnant because I didn't want to raise my children alone.

Although my family was around me, I still felt alone. I felt like I had to prove that I could be a good mother on my own, without relying on my parents. I always focused on taking care of the twins and all my responsibilities, but I lived with suppressed frustration. I had it all together on the surface, but inside I was falling apart. I wanted to find the balance to be the best mother I could be.

"Babygirl, let being a mom always be your first job. Don't worry about anything else", Daddy reminds me. The guidance of my parents has helped me when facing life obstacles. Many of my friends had one parent in their home. I feel blessed to have had both of them with me. Although sometimes it was overwhelming having two disciplinarians, it made me better. Watching my parents navigate family and parenting gives me a firm foundation. My parents are strict but also fun and loving. Having both parents gave me social and emotional support. My mom cooked and maintained the home and the structure of the chores. My dad was the go-to for speeches of all sorts: detailed instructions on doing something or discipline when grades were low.

I can remember my mom cooking for us. She made the best oatmeal and cream of wheat. She would have us in the kitchen during the holidays to learn how to cook. My parents always ensured we had everything we needed to the best of their ability, and I was determined to do the same for my children. Watching my mom give instructions to us and being systematic with things around the house like chores, bedtime, and downtime was very helpful when I became a mother. Growing up, we were given specific tasks to complete by a particular time. If we didn't do our chores, my mom would fuss or punish us before saying, "wait till your dad gets home." When my dad got home at midnight, he would wake us up to do our chores.

One time Sierra didn't do the dishes, and she would always drink his soda. This night he woke us up, and the six of us had to line up in front of him. "Who was supposed to do the dishes?" No one said anything. We all looked at Sierra. "Who drank my soda and put water in it? "At this point, I knew we would be in big trouble. Daddy loves his soda. Still, nobody said anything. We would fight amongst ourselves, but we stuck together and, most importantly, didn't tell on each other. This unity drove my parents crazy, but at the same time, it made them very happy to know that we stick together no matter what. "Oh, y'all gonna stand together, and ain't nobody gonna say who did it?" He sent us to stand outside on the porch until we figured out who did it. Of course, Faniesha did not want to stand out there with us. She said if Sierra didn't confess, she would tell. Daddy opened the door and said, "now, are y'all ready to talk?" Of course, we said yes. It's the middle of the night, and it's cold outside.

Inside the house, we are lined up again. "Talk," he says. We are all looking at Sierra. She still didn't say anything. My dad says, "Ok, everyone is about to get a spanking." Nope, that wasn't going to happen. Faniesha says, "it was Sierra." Daddy sent the rest of us to bed, Sierra had to wash the dishes, and she got disciplined alone. We stood together against our parents all the time, as a team, unless there was the threat of a spanking. Some people will say that's child abuse, but with six teenage kids, my parents were creative with discipline.

Once I became a mother, I gained a new perspective on the power of words. In hindsight, I was afraid to tell my parents I was pregnant because of what I heard Ma say. "I will kill you if you get pregnant." I grew from this by understanding that those words were to impart fear, but how much fear do I want my children to have? I had a respectful fear of my parents, but this fear created distance when facing life challenges.

Big Granma believed that sparing the rod spoils the child. My parents held to this too, but I changed it a bit with my children. The old-school way is to do as I say and not worry about what I'm doing. I choose to lead by example. I bring that to the forefront and ensure my children have a voice. I teach them that their thoughts and opinions count, and I want them to be unafraid to share with me. I believe this gives children a firmer foundation in communication. I create a safe place for my children to express themselves and work through their mistakes. I am careful of my words, so my twins know I have their back no matter what, like my parents. Even if I speak or act out of frustration or anger, it is rooted in love.

In the beauty industry, styles are like a revolving door, and when it comes around, it's often tweaked a bit. When clients bring me pictures of popular techniques, I have to make adjustments to execute the look successfully for them. Different factors include facial structure, head shape, lifestyle, hairline, and hair texture. These all affect the proper styling execution. As parents, we mimic what we observe our parents do and make tweaks intentionally and sometimes without realizing it. Now that I am over 20 years into parenting, I often mimic when parenting my children. Some parenting strategies I adopted from my parents and others I have changed, not because those ways are wrong, but because I gained a new perspective.

I encourage you to talk to them from birth if you have children. This teaches them to converse with you from the beginning. At all the textures and phases of life, communication is essential. In their earlier years, they are listening intently. They become more expressive and verbal when they are preteens and life is wavy. I intentionally sat down and had conversations with them about all kinds of things. Teenagers need guidance and consistency in communication in this stage. They face significant changes and must have space to communicate how they feel.

Having communication takes a great deal of creativity. Each child is different. Love your child for who and where they are, and encourage them to be the best version of themselves possible. Be honest with them and challenge them to be honest with themselves. Help them know how to speak their truth with respect and still honor their parents simultaneously. There's no one way to parent a child. With each experience, you face many different challenges, which is what makes having children fun. There's a level of adventure that comes with it.

## CHAPTER 6

# A Growing Family

During my first year with the twins, I began doing hair from the house and gradually developed a clientele of women and men in the church. An usher named Jay took notice and kept asking every Sunday if his hair was long enough to style. It was not. Jay is a tall, brown-skinned man who has a round stomach but wears it well. He was very well-dressed all the time. If he wasn't in a suit, he had on freshly ironed slacks with a nice button-down shirt and some soft bottom shoes. Jay has a wavy texture of hair. Although it's high density, his strands are medium in diameter. Once his hair finally grew long enough to style, it was easy to create styles. He went from flat twist to cornrows in about six months.

Jay had the perfect personality for an usher. He engages with everyone whether he's known them for a long time or if they are strangers. He would greet people with a smile and, most times, a joke because he loved making people laugh. I was annoyed by him. We met as teenagers in the S.W.A.T (Students With A Testimony) ministry. I didn't like him when we were teenagers either. One time, he had to give my brothers and me a ride home after a S.W.A.T event. He was so belligerent and extra Riding in the car with him at 17 years old, I said, "I feel sorry for whoever ends up with him"...ironically, I did.

My parents bought a new house with four bedrooms, three upstairs and one downstairs. There was a two-car driveway and a yard big enough for all the grandchildren to run around and play, but I liked the yard at our old house better. We made epic memories there. A split foyer at the entrance leads to an eat-in kitchen and dining room, a full laundry room, and a patio. Ma and Daddy were happy to move into the home they always wanted for us. They planned a housewarming party and told us to invite everyone.

My brothers wanted Jay to come to the housewarming but refused to invite him. One Sunday, we argued about who would ask him for his number. My brothers said asking another guy for his number wasn't okay. It made no sense, but I gave in, even though I knew he might think I was asking for myself. Donnell tells me to call Jay and invite him a few days later. "Wait, what?" I responded. All I was supposed to do was get his number. You all never said I had to call". They say it's weird for a guy to invite another guy over. We argued again, and I gave in again. I made the call, and I am on the phone with Jay, and my brothers are on the line. We talked and laughed for a bit. I finally said my brothers wanted to ask you to come to their gathering, and he said yes. Shortly after, my brothers got off the phone, but we kept talking for almost three hours. He was in the men's choir and enjoyed singing and good music, so we had that in common. He was still living with his mother but working as a substitute teacher and got hired at Metro as a bus operator. After I hung up, I felt like he wasn't so bad.

I get home late. It's Saturday, the salon's busiest day, and the housewarming is tonight. As soon as I walk in, Jay is the first to say something to me. "How are you going to invite someone to your house and not be there when they arrive?" This is exactly why I didn't want to be the one to invite him. I laugh it off and say, "Umm, no, you are my brother's company." I say hello to everyone before excusing myself. After working all day, I am ready for a shower. I love the fragrance of baby powder, and I always wear it.

Jay said I smelled like a newborn baby when I rejoined everyone downstairs. I chuckled. The rest of the night, he made every joke about me. It was cute. We all enjoyed talking, joking, and laughing at the housewarming party. It was getting late, and his mom was ready to go, but a bunch of us were still hanging out. My brothers told Jay he could just drop his mom off and return, reassuring him we weren't going anywhere. He took his mother home and returned to us all talking, watching movies, and making lots of jokes. I love to laugh, and Jay knows how to make people laugh. As everyone headed home, he asked me to walk him to the door. I didn't expect what he would say next, "I think I like you, but I'm not sure. I just got out of a relationship, and I don't want this just to be a rebound".

We started talking on the phone all the time. I don't remember our first date, but we began to spend a lot of time together. We kept our relationship just between us. He was surprisingly romantic. Taking care of my children, working full time, and dating was hard to balance, but he was very understanding. He would usually pick me up from work and see me at the salon. We found a way to make it work. It was fun dating, Jay. He was different from what I thought of him as the annoying usher. I felt like I could talk to him about anything. He understood my unique way of seeing the world when no one else did. He even taught me how to drive. Well, him and my brother Garry. They got on my last nerve while teaching me, but I finally got my driver's license at 24.

After a year of dating, Jay got his apartment. We got a U-Haul and helped him move his belongings. When we brought down a China cabinet, we were careful not to break the glass doors while navigating three flights of stairs. The tape breaks as soon as we get it onto the truck, the tape breaks, and one of the doors flips out. It hits the truck and breaks. Jay hopped out of the truck and jumped up and down in the middle of the street. He looked like a kid having a temper tantrum. He was so upset because the glass door broke after making it down all those steps. We were able to laugh it off.

Once he got settled, I helped him put together a housewarming party. People started arriving while I was in the kitchen preparing food. My hair is undone, and I haven't changed my clothes yet. He called me out of the kitchen, grabbed the twins, and put them on my lap. At first, I didn't know what was happening, but I realized as he began to talk. Tears filled my eyes while he was down on his knee, holding my hand. "Will you marry me?" I look at my twins. The looks on their faces assured me that they were okay with me saying yes. I said yes, and he put the ring on my finger. Jay turned to my twins and asked if he could be their dad. My Ladybug had a look on her face that said, "No sir, I'm good." It wasn't until he pulled out a box, opened it, and saw the gold earrings that she said, "oh yes, you can be my dad now." Everyone laughed about it. I was so overwhelmed with joy.

My parents approved of us getting married, but they did wish we'd dated a little longer. From our engagement until our wedding four months later, Jay's mother made it known she did not want us to get married. According to her, I was just looking for someone to father my twins. She called me out of my name many times and even compared me to a dune buggy, which is not a car, but only a shell of a car. So disrespectful. Jay is her only son and child, so I understand her not letting him go. She caused so many unnecessary frustrations, but I love her son.

I arrived at the church late because my mom and sister were bossing me so much. My dress was perfect: off-white, the sheer sleeves that flowed over my hands with hand-sewn jewels and crystal work. Every detail was a work of art. The day was so wonderful. It was more than I could have imagined.

The twins were well-behaved, but I was afraid that the hustle and bustle of the day would get to them. Although they were very respectful children, they had their moments. The twins are so sharp. Fatboy in his little off-white tuxedo, he and Jay, had on the same tuxedo with wine-colored vest and ties, and their shoes were so shiny off-white too. My brother Donnell was Jay's best man, and my sisters Teresa and Faniesha were my maids of honor. JJ was responsible for the music during our service. He wrote a special song for me and my dad, his rendition of the *Butterfly Kisses* by Bob Dylan. It brought me to tears during the service. My mom made all the flower arrangements and decorations and put gold and wine-colored decorations on Ladybug's dress. The tall centerpieces for the tables were floral with off-white and wine-colored flowers in the vases paired with small arrangements and floating candles. It was like something out of a magazine.

My family was excited and happy for me. I believe they saw how happy I was, and that's all that mattered to them. My joy was at the center of that day. Big Granma was very excited for me, and I was so happy she could celebrate with me. She always pushed me to love from a place that I couldn't even understand at that moment, but I do now. My family embraced Jay with open arms. The one thing we enjoyed was our family getting more members added. So, he was the sure sign of our family getting bigger, and he enjoyed having family around him, so that was a huge plus.

When it was time to walk down the aisle, Tonya, the chef who catered our wedding, walked past and said, "Hey... y'all look so good. How does it feel to be giving away your baby girl?" My dad teared up. I looked into his eyes and said, "Daddy, don't cry. I'm not going far." He began to cry. I had never seen him cry before. I saw him sad but never in tears. I could see how much he loved me. This moment warmed my heart, and I felt the deepest connection to him.

On my wedding day, I refused to let anything steal my joy. It was a bittersweet moment to have all my siblings there except Sierra. During the reception, I spoke to Jay's mother. I told her that I loved her and appreciated her. She was surprised, but I wanted to show her the love of Christ.

After we married, life was very peaceful. The transition was smooth because the twins go with the flow and do well with change. I focused on being the best wife and mom I could be. Having a blended family is not easy. The twins had to get used to having Jay play a part in their growth and development. My husband went from having no children to having two thriving young children. While life felt so rewarding with my "perfect family." We found our rhythm and flowed in it. That first year was dreamy. We functioned well as a family unit, and I was excited about the future.

We wanted to have children. We tried for three years to get pregnant. Just when you stop trying, it always happens. After I was married, I joined the dance ministry. We were in the middle of ministering, and my back went out. I had to go to the emergency room. After blood work, the doctor comes in to tell me that I'm eight weeks pregnant. We were shocked but thrilled, and the twins were excited about having a new baby in the house. This was an exciting time for us. This pregnancy wasn't easy, but we had our baby girl in August.

Four months later, I found out I was pregnant again. This pregnancy had some complications. Although I had gestational diabetes, I kept it under control. But my feet and left leg would go numb, and I continuously had premature contractions. The doctors told me the complications were because of the baby's position three weeks before my due date. I was constantly going to the hospital because of my contractions. I was instructed to come in only if my contractions were five minutes apart, and I did. After getting checked in, the nurse connects me to the monitors before the doctor comes in. He looks at the activity of my contractions, and although they are five minutes apart, he says they will need to stop the contractions. I took medication, and the contractions stopped. The nurse says they will bring my discharge papers shortly. I waited about 10 minutes. I was ready to go home. I asked for the nurse, but she still had me waiting. I finished getting myself ready and proceeded to leave. When I left the room and began to walk down the hall, they tried to stop me. The nurse said I needed to sign my papers and get my discharge instructions. I replied, "I don't need any instructions because I followed your last discharge instructions and ended up right back here in the same position." I walked out. Two days later, the cramps returned.

I'm awakened to a baby girl crying in her crib, a baby in my stomach. I could not walk to attend to my baby. My only option was to crawl through the pain. I sat up on my bed and managed to make it to the floor. As I moved through the five steps, it felt like fifty while I held onto everything I could to support me until I could get up.

I called my doctor, and he told me to call the specialist. I called the specialist. The specialist said, "Why isn't he sending you to the hospital? There's not much I can do, but come in, and I will check on you and the baby. Even at one year-old, my baby girl was very helpful. It was almost like she could sense I wasn't feeling well on this day. Her clothes were on the end of my bed, and after I cleaned her up, she walked over and began putting her clothes on. I struggled to put my clothes on, and she said, "Mommy, I will help you." I can hardly stand the pain while getting her in the stroller. I managed to get myself and my baby girl dressed, but getting to the car was a struggle. I finally reached the doctor's office and got to the elevator. Thankfully, I had the stroller to help me. They took me to the exam room, and shortly after, the technician told me she would get the doctor. I know this can't be good from experience and the look on her face.

The doctor takes several images of the baby. All I could hear was the keys on the computer clicking. All I could feel was the probe rolling across my stomach. After several minutes, the doctor says, "it's time for your baby to be born. I am calling your doctor. I need you to go straight to the hospital. Don't stop anywhere. Go straight to the hospital. Have someone meet you there to get the baby."

After getting dressed, I pushed the stroller to the waiting area and called my mom. She didn't want me to drive myself and convinced me to stay at the doctor's office. Jay agreed that I didn't need to drive, but I insisted. As I make it to the front of the building, Ma pulls up at the entrance. I don't know how she got to the office so fast, but I'm glad. If she weren't, I would have driven myself. When we arrived at the hospital, the nurse connected me to the baby to the monitors. She examined me and asked intake questions. As she was feeling the baby, she asked, "how many pounds did they say she was going to be?" I say 7 pounds, but she estimated about 9 or 10 pounds. Soon, they began the induction process, and the pain was extreme. There were some points where I couldn't breathe.

When I was dilated enough to get the epidural, I was relieved. Once I got it, there was this feeling of pressure, not pain. For me, the epidural only worked on one side. So although I had relief on my right side, the pain on the left side I could feel throughout the whole side of my body. The doctor altered the epidural, and there was still no relief. As time passed, the pain subsided more, but my water wouldn't break, so the doctor had to break it manually. This felt really weird, but shortly afterward, it was time to push moments later. The nurse comes to the head of my bed on my left side. Jay is excited and ready to meet his baby girl, and our mothers are on my right, prepared to meet another grandbaby. The doctor is at the foot of the bed, and I am positioned to push her out. "PUSH! BREATHE! WAIT....DON'T PUSH YET!" I can hear as I slowly feel a sharp surge of pain pulse through my body.

The nurse turned off my epidural, and the doctor told me I needed to handle the contractions so that they could direct me on when to push.

She was coming. I could feel her. I could feel her head was out, but she was not moving anymore as I continued pushing. "Get the forceps" He intended to grab my baby's head and twist her out because her shoulder was stuck. "NO, I will push harder." You know he did it anyway. I was grateful I pushed more, so he didn't need to twist her much. Her shoulder was free, and she was out. They rushed her to clean up, but I didn't hear her crying. This is way too long for her not to cry. I took a deep sigh of relief; her cry was music to my ears.

During childbirth, the contractions are and will always be the most intense pain a woman can experience. But these contractions help your beautiful baby join you in the world. All three of my labors were induced. It was because Ladybug's umbilical cord was wrapped around her neck twice with the twins. Flip wasn't moving, and her fluids were low, so they decided I needed to be induced. Bunny was even more complicated. I had contractions, but hours went by, and my water did not break on its own. The doctor decided to help labor by using a tool to break it. Although I have never experienced my water breaking, I can tell you it's quite a bit of fluid.

"Oh my goodness, look at her dimples." Everyone in the room was rushing around. The moment of utter joy was short before it turned into complete worry. She weighed 12lbs and 3oz, and they took her straight to the NICU. While I get stitched up, Ma and Jay's mom start arguing. Something that happened in the waiting area spilled over into my room. The nurse kindly asked them to leave. "Babygirl, I'm sorry, but you know how I am about my twins." Ma didn't play when it came to her grandchildren or us. When she disrespected me, I never said anything to her. I always respected her as Jay's mother. Ma had enough and reminded her that I didn't need to look for a father for my children because Daddy was a father figure to all of us.

Split Ends must be cut off, and so must negativity. Cut it off. Split ends will cause you to lose more hair if left alone. When negativity tries to creep in, CUT IT OFF. Those who embrace negativity and spin it into a positive are the ones that are truly successful in life.

When we got to the NICU, I saw my baby girl with the deepest dimples ever. I'm so sad because I still can't hold her. I couldn't rest, knowing I couldn't touch my child. The nurses kept telling me that she was ok and to rest. They explained that she needed to be checked and tested for certain things because of her size.

I was able to get a little sleep, but my back was sore from the epidural. The pain didn't stop me from going to see my baby. As I walked the hallways, I heard the nurses talking about the 12-pound baby pushed out last night. I continued to visit the NICU, and finally, I was able to feed and bond with her. The nurses brought her to me a few times as well. They wanted to keep her for a little further observation, and I was not leaving the hospital without my baby. The nurse noted that she was only eating 3oz. I was so angry. "She is a newborn. How much do you think she should be eating?" I cried so hard my eyes were swollen. I thought I would have to leave the hospital without my baby, but my doctor told me that I would be able to stay until they released her. A few days later, we were home. My baby girl wore a heart monitor that recorded her heart and lung function. After about three months we didn't have to use it anymore.

Our family expanded from two children to four, so a two-bedroom apartment was insufficient. We moved into my childhood home. My parents were able to keep the house and rent it out. The twins were excited because they could go outside more often to play. Having a big yard to play in was a plus for them. Fatboy quickly adapted to his new siblings, but Ladybug was very different. She always talked about wishing she was an only child. I had to get creative with her. I spoke to her about why it seemed like I spent more time and gave more attention to them. I wanted her to feel attended to, so I offered to help her do things like getting dressed, and she said no every time.

As our family of four dynamic settled, the twins expressed that they felt like I was doing everything for the girls and that I didn't spend enough time with them. So to get them to understand, I showed them that the babies' needs differ from theirs. For a week, they saw all I had to do for the girls daily. They started offering to get them dressed. The icing on the cake was when I sat at the table and began to feed them. Ladybug said, "Mommy, you know we can do this ourselves." At that moment, I could now explain what I had been doing all week. I told them that the girls needed me more than they did because I had already taught them how to do things that I now have to teach them. Ladybug helped Flip and Fatboy helped Bunny. It just happened that way. They are all very close, and Fatboy is an amazing brother to the 3 of them. After that, I had no problems, and they became a big help with caring for the girls and teaching them how to do things. To this day, the twins help guide the girls, teaching them things and helping them understand mistakes they made growing up.

## CHAPTER 7

# The Pain at its Highest

It began as a regular day. I'm working from home doing hair for a family friend. My twins are in their bedroom, and my baby girls play on the floor next to us. Mrs. Violet and I were talking when my phone rang. All I heard was fear and strain in my mother's voice. "It's your father. Something is wrong. He is not breathing. I need you to come. I need help".

Mrs. Violet said she would stay with my children. Jay was still at work, and it was almost time for him to get off. I called him on my drive to meet my mother at Landover Subway station. I had no idea what was going on or if my dad would be ok. I remember my heart racing. When I arrived, I saw an ambulance and my mom crying and screaming for them to help. The EMTs put him into the back of the ambulance. We could see the paramedics inside, but they didn't pull off. They sat there for five long minutes, and we screamed for them to pull off the entire time. They finally drove off, just as Faniesha came out of the train station in shock. We rush to the hospital, and Jay is there, but we must wait when we arrive. The doctor announces that my dad has passed. From this point, things are blurry.

I can recall sitting in the waiting area near where they had my dad in a room. One by one, family members came. They asked where he was with tears in their eyes, where he was, and I would point to the room where my mom sat next to his body, crying. I was numb. Everyone wanted to know what had happened. I tried to explain, but the pain ran so deep through me that it was difficult to speak. Jay was supportive at the hospital. He doesn't listen to many men, but he has a great deal of respect for Daddy. He would listen when my dad discussed things with him or made suggestions. Jay loved my dad as his father. I appreciated seeing growth in their relationship. He knew that my dad was my strength. He kept telling me that he was there and that it would be ok. Whenever I heard someone say that, all I could think was, *No, it's not; my dad is gone. Nothing will be the same again.*

Driving home from the hospital, I couldn't stop crying. I didn't know how I was going to tell my children. Daddy was more than a grandfather. He cared for my twins like a father. I parked and took a moment to collect myself. I walk into the house, and Mrs. Violet is there holding my baby girl, who was four months old at the time. She had already heard the news and said, "I am here for you." I called the twins downstairs. Ladybug says, "Mommy, what's wrong." I take a deep breath, "Your grandfather passed."

There are no words to describe the look in their eyes. "What did you just say?" they asked. I had to repeat it. They began to cry. Jay walked in the door as I was telling them. He couldn't say anything. Jay just stood there. I could see he was in disbelief that daddy was gone. There was not much to say at that moment. He didn't have any words for us, not even a joke. Mrs. Violet and I gave them comfort. There was nothing I could do to make them feel better. I held them close, assuring them that he was much better now. There were times when the children saw Daddy when he wasn't doing too well, so they understood me.

Before he passed, Daddy had a few preexisting health conditions, including diabetes, high blood pressure, and heart failure. He had triple bypass surgery a few years prior and was very sick. It took him about three months to recover. I remember when he came home; Daddy had a heart-shaped pillow that helped him when he coughed so he did not jolt his incision. Daddy pushed hard to recover and control his high blood pressure and diabetes so that he could be there for us. He got better, so we thought. We learned he was in much more pain than he allowed us to see.

Doctors told Daddy his heart was only working at 30% when I was in high school. He never told us but continued to smile, joke, and live life to the fullest no matter how he felt physically. My father showed me that you don't have to succumb to physical pain; it takes strength to do this. I believe he is without pain now, and I wanted my children to hold on to that; even though we all preferred, he still is here with us. I figured them grasping that Granddad was without pain now could ease the pain they felt in his absence.

We all gathered at my parents' house the next day and began planning my father's funeral: Ma, all six children, sixteen grandchildren, and three great-grandchildren. We were at the house every day until the service, and we cried together. We sometimes talked about my dad, the joys of having him around, and the legacy he left with us. I watched Daddy and Ma work hard over the years to accomplish the goals they set for the family. Daddy's philosophy in all that he faced was never to give up and learn from anything you go through. He said your failures are not failures but a step towards your goal.

Although my dad had insurance, my mom had to wait before receiving the money. Our church graciously covered the funeral costs, and my mother repaid them later. It was so rewarding to know that Daddy was a loving man to us at his funeral and to everyone.

For several weeks after the funeral, we went with my mom. Sometimes it wasn't all of us, but all of us gave support and comfort to her. I had to support so many other people during that time, so it was a while before I stopped to accept that he was no longer here. Grieving has been a slow process. Sometimes I'm crushed that I can't see, hear, sit, or talk to him about my troubles. Writing about this is healing. I always say that I'm ok even when I'm not one-hundred percent. I have permitted myself to grieve. I experienced depression these past few weeks while revisiting this part of my past. Here it is ten years later, and through my writing, I finally faced the loss of my dad. It was like I took a trip back in time. I am feeling the pain as if it just happened.

For months my toes went numb. Every morning I had to shake my feet before driving to feel the pedals. Strapping the babies into their car seats triggered extreme numbness in my feet. It felt like a bunch of tiny needles like I hit my funny bone. Oh, the discomfort! I moved through it, of course. I am a mother, wife, cosmetologist, and at that time, a full-time student. I decided to return to cosmetology school shortly after my dad passed. He was so encouraging and supportive when it came to me finishing school. I told my husband that I wanted my hair license, and I went back to school with his support.

When I was 21, I finished all the tests and required hours, but somehow it was undocumented. I was expecting to get release paperwork to take my license test, but they told me I had almost 200 hours to finish. I was stubborn and refused to go back because I knew I had done all my hours. I had two children and needed to work, not sit in a class, and redo the hours I had already completed. With my skill and professionalism, I made it work for years. I did hair from home and obtained chairs at numerous shops. No one ever asked for my hair license. My reputation preceded me.

About a month into school, my grandmother passed. She was the spice of our family. She gave it to you straight and took care of us all. While my dad's death was sudden and surprising, we knew she would be leaving us soon; but that still didn't take away from the pain. She was my very first client. As a small girl, I loved brushing and oiling her hair. Big Granma's hair was mostly white with a little black mixed into the back. Her hair was so soft and curly. She didn't have much hair on the top, which is why she always wanted it combed up. I guess you could call it a comb-over. She fostered my talent for hair grooming. Big Granma's presence is still strong. She was a very hard-working woman. From watching her, I learned how to walk with confidence and never apologize for anything I choose to do for myself. Her words are gold, and she always gave me advice and perspective. The twins spent a lot of time with Big Granma for their first three years, and she poured into them. I am thankful for the lessons she taught me and the lessons they learned from her.

My morning routine consisted of getting the kids up and dressed, which was seldom easy with 10-year-old twins, a one-year-old, and an infant. I make breakfast, and I finish getting myself ready while they are eating. I drop them off at my mother's, and I'm on my way to school. After school, I head to work and stay until 6 or 7, depending on the day. I pick up the kids to go home and start the next day again. Jay wasn't part of the morning routine because his work schedule didn't allow him to be. After school and work, I would pick the kids up from my mom, then drive home, about a two-hour commute. Once I got home, I had to get the kids settled. Sometimes I would fix a small snack for the twins, but I had to give the babies something before they went to bed because if not, they would wake up in the middle of the night. Before the twins settled into bed, I would check homework and read with them. Sometimes I couldn't read with them, so Jay would help settle them and read with them. Then, I would have a little downtime, but I chose to study most of the time.

One morning I couldn't move. There was a sharp pain from my back to my toes. No matter how hard I tried, I couldn't stand up. My twins dressed the babies while I called my mom to help. My mom drove the children to school, and I got an appointment with my doctor. It took a while, but I could get together and drive to the doctor. I tend to ignore any pain or discomfort that doesn't stop me from moving, but I couldn't move that morning.

My mind was racing. What is happening with my legs? In the exam room, I tell the doctor about the numbness and the pain. As I continued to tell the doctor about other issues, she said, "It sounds like spinal stenosis, but let's get an MRI done so we can see what's going on." I lay in this loud tube-like machine. They gave me earplugs to buffer the noise, but they didn't work. Even in the loudness, I wondered what spinal stenosis looked like and how I could have gotten it. I thought about all the moments of pain I ignored leading up to this morning. I had to wait a few days for the MRI results, and Jay took off from work to take me to the appointment. The doctor placed the images on the board and explained what we saw. The photos showed my spinal canal was narrow, which indicates stenosis or arthritis of the spine. The many follow-up appointments revealed the cause. In all three of my pregnancies, I carried 9+ pounds. Doing hair had put stress on the back as well.

Over the next few months, I bought better shoes and visited several specialists to figure out what to do for the numbness and pain in my back and feet. I tried so many medications. None of them worked. Most of them made me very sick. One time I took a new pain medication that the doctor said would not make me drowsy, which was important because I wanted to care for my children. Out of nowhere, my face was numb, my lips felt weird, and I was trying to feed my baby. I called Jay, and I told him something was wrong. I didn't know what was happening. I felt like I was getting ready to slob on myself. He told me to give my baby Bunny to Ladybug and lay down because I was high. This wasn't the last time I would feel like this. Being a mom was my most important job. The reality is I had two other roles that were equally important to me.

As a wife, I began to feel like I was failing. I couldn't iron Jay's uniforms and cook as I had before. I always wanted him to know how much I adored him and appreciated how hard he worked, so I always ensured he had minimal pressure when he came home from work. I couldn't relieve that pressure anymore because I was in so much pain I needed help around the house and with the kids. Some people felt I gave him too much and did too much to make it easy for him. In my opinion, that is what a wife is supposed to do for her husband. But I needed his help, and he still had to go to work for long hours. I felt like I was a burden on him at times. Although I know he understood, I could see and feel his frustration with the family dynamics change.

The art of hair is my skill, and my love and care for the people I service is my gift. Not giving people the level of joy they experienced through my service was surprisingly very difficult. At this point, I learned how passionate I was about the beauty industry. Seeing a person's face who just got a new hairdo was the most rewarding thing. I still had friends and clients come to the house and sit on the floor to get their hair done. They told me they didn't want anyone else doing their hair. So, they shampooed their hair. I would style it. A few of them brought me some big pillows to put on the floor for their comfort. Sometimes it would be 3-4 of them coming over to visit. It would be a time of laughter, food, drinks, and me doing hair. I also realized how much my clients loved me as a friend. They would come over with dinner for the kids and play with them while I fixed them up and were patient if I needed a break.

Soon, my pain increased so severely that I had to take another break from school to give the energy I had to provide for my family. I was just a few months away from finishing but in too much pain to continue. I felt defeated, like no matter how hard I pushed myself or how many of life's hurdles I jumped over, I continuously hit a wall.

The pain was extreme, and I wanted to do more for my family. Although these were hard times, my family kept me from giving in to the pain. It's because of them I knew that I needed to keep walking. I learned that if you don't move, you won't move. Although arthritis is painful, moving through the pain is helpful. The pain lessens the more you move through it. My dad and grandmother are still with me. Their words of wisdom guide me, and their spirits live through me.

# CHAPTER 8

# A New Spine

After many ER visits, I was referred to an excellent doctor. I made an appointment and collected all my images and paperwork dealing with my back. Most times, it was just my girls (Flip & Bunny) in the car and me, and that ride to the doctor's office was no different. We listened to music, and they danced in their car seats. Hearing their little voices sing and seeing them in the rearview mirror always filled me with joy. I got them in the double stroller when we arrived at the office. They had a lot of energy at one and two, so the double was essential. I signed in, sat, and played with the girls, so the wait passed quickly. I gathered the girls and their winter coats and pushed them into the exam room. I was ready to give them the images of my spine, but the nurse told me the doctor wanted current ones. While I changed and got new images, the nurse watched the girls, and when I returned, my girls were waiting with smiles that warmed me. The nurse said the doctor would be in shortly. Well, her 'shortly' was long, and I waited thirty minutes in that room. To my surprise, I began to worry about the girls getting fussy and hungry, but they were very calm and patient.

When the doctor finally arrived, he introduced himself, and we talked briefly about all that led me to see him. I explained that I was tired of the pain medication. I hated feeling high. I couldn't take care of my babies. I could not continue to function this way. When I let the medication take over, I truly understood what it means to disconnect from reality. The pain was only gone for a moment. That was the most incredible feeling until the moment was over. Once I came down from the high, the reality was still there. I was still in pain. My body wasn't doing what my mind wanted it to do.

The doctor explained that I had spinal stenosis, which I already knew. He said that a bone in my lower back was rubbing up against nerves in my lumbar. This is why the medication was no relief, causing other issues for me. A few weeks before this appointment, I started experiencing incontinence of my bowels and bladder—one of the worst experiences I have ever had. I wasn't feeling the urge to use the bathroom until it was too late. And because I had extreme pain in my back, I would need help cleaning myself up if I had an accident. Jay and my twins would help me. It was mortifying to have them see me like that. I was so blessed that my oldest daughter would help me without hesitation or complaint. At times I couldn't finish taking a shower because my pain increased. She would help me get out of the shower, rinse off, and get dressed.

I was trying to process that the bone on my nerves was the source of all the issues. The doctor explained that I needed emergency surgery because of my symptoms and the incontinence issue, which can become permanent. He scheduled me to go into surgery the following day.

*I need to set up things for the kids. Who is going to get them to school? Who is going to take care of my babies? Is Jay going to be ok by himself with all four children?* So many thoughts began to run through my head. So many questions that I didn't have answers to. Everything started moving so fast. I will go into lumbar fusion surgery tomorrow so the doctor can decompress and remove the bone causing my pain.

I was in the doctor's office for two hours, and the nurses were with me every step. When the nurse returned, I had tried my best not to cry in front of my baby girls. I felt heartbroken looking at their little smiling faces as they sat and played on the exam table. I was worried if I'd be able to walk after the surgery, and already struggling to take care of my household. The nurse offered to take the babies for a moment while I filled out paperwork. After I finished my appointment, I registered for emergency surgery, and one of the nurses stayed to make sure I didn't need further assistance with the girls. When she left, another nurse came to assist me while I completed more paperwork and tests in preparation for the surgery. At times, my girls got a bit fussy, but for the most part, they were very patient through it all.

I called my family to tell them what was happening and headed home. It was a thirty-minute drive, but it felt like hours. My mind was heavy. Once I pulled up to the front of our house, the girls were asleep. So, I just sat there until they woke up. I'm thinking about how my twins will feel and how my babies will be cared for. I dreaded telling them about my having surgery in less than 24 hours. I never got out of the car. When the girls woke up, I just started the car again and went to pick the twins up from my mom's house. *How do I say this without crushing them? Breathe, just Breathe and say the words.*

"This is not easy for me to say...Mommy has to have surgery tomorrow". I reminded them of all the issues I'd been having and explained that I would feel better after the surgery. As a family, we had to figure things out fast. My mom and Jay contacted the church, and so many church members could help in different ways.

The following day, I checked in and got prepped for surgery. I changed into a hospital gown, put all my belongings in a bag, and gave them to Jay. The nurse told me they were not responsible for losing any personal items. I remember this made me a little nervous because I always had my dad's bracelet on me. The doctor explained how the next few hours would go. My surgery would be four hours, and they would give my family updates. There were only two people in the operating room at first: the anesthesiologist and a nurse in the operating room. This kept me calm. As the anesthesiologist explained how I would feel in the next few minutes, I noticed several people entering the room. He released the medication into my IV and told me to count backward from 10. There were too many people moving around me to trust, and I felt my body positioned on the table.

Waking up from surgery was painful; I didn't remember falling asleep. Initially, the doctors planned to do a 2-level fusion, but they winded up doing a 3-level fusion. My surgery took eighteen hours because my bones are incredibly dense. I was in rehab for over a week, and it was not as hard as I thought it would be. Jay and my girls visited throughout the week, and because of school, my twins came on the weekend.

It has always been difficult for me to ask for help, which I am working on. There is something inside that stops me. Even in rehab, while I learned how to do things with my new back, I didn't ask for help. I spoke with my therapist twice a day during my week of recovery. One day, I was in so much pain that I refused my morning therapy session. I hated how the medication made me feel, and I didn't want to take more, so I just laid there. During my afternoon session, I explained that the pain was unbearable. As we talked, she challenged my thinking and understanding of pain. "Just keep moving through the pain. "Feel it. Sit in it. Wait for it to subside. If we allow ourselves to feel the pain, and in that discomfort keep moving, ultimately we learn to navigate the pain". The pain I felt that morning was still there, but I took her advice and intentionally moved through it. Whether the pain is emotional, physical, or mental, I encourage you to push through. Keep moving, no matter how hard it gets or how bad it hurts.

Coming home from rehab was an adjustment. We had moved back into my childhood home, and I couldn't navigate the steps well.

Cleaning and caring for the children was still a challenge some days. In addition, I revisited the emotional strain of being in my childhood home with the constant reminders of my sexual assault and my dad's passing. Walking through the memories of that day and finally releasing the hurt connected to it. This is where I was living when I had my very first surgery. I'm grateful for being there to bring myself to a place to recognize where I needed counseling and emotional healing.

Jay put a bed in the living room so I could lay down like I needed to. Each day of recovery started with pain medication. My twins were old enough to get up independently, and Ladybug helped me and the girls get dressed if Jay couldn't. He would drop off the children at school, and afterward, they would go to my parent's house. We didn't have childcare during the day, so my Bunny stayed with me on the bed and laid behind my legs. Jay or the twins would prepare her milk and food for the day, so I didn't have to do much. If I fell asleep because of the medication, she would stay on the bed behind my legs until I woke up. Other times, my mother or Jay's mother would take care of her until Jay could pick her up. It was challenging to create a routine after the surgery. I never knew what my body would feel like when I woke up.

My memories of this time are cloudy, but certain things remain so clear to me, like having to use a bedside commode or struggling up the stairs to take a shower. I had to wash off in the living room for a few days. I could not cook or help with homework because I was so sleepy from the pain medication. During this time, I couldn't play with my baby girls, care for them, or teach them the way I was able to with the twins. Being a mom and not being able to mother was so crushing.

My friend Angela is the girl's godmother. She really understood me, and even though I never asked for help, she knew when to step in and give support. Her high energy and no-nonsense attitude were great for me. Angela knew when to push me to open up, which is hard to find in a friend. I am very closed, especially when I'm going through hard times. Angela, just like T, would always show up. Lisa, Ivory, and many other women in the church came to support me, making sure the girl's educational development continued. Christen, Kendra, and Kenya came to cook, clean, and nurture my children. My sister-in-law Miama took care of my baby girls as her own. She would stay with me during the day, ensuring I had meals and helping me whenever I needed them. While recovering from surgery, I learned to trust and let people into my personal space. I still struggle with trusting people, but I have learned to recognize who my "tribe" is.

There was a sense of normalcy as I got stronger, although some days were still tough. It took about a year for me to feel fully recovered. I was able to drive the kids to school and go grocery shopping. Some may take these simple things for granted. I could walk around the store for 30 minutes to get food for my family. I know life without that luxury.

I returned to school and earned my certification in makeup artistry and my hair license. Although my physical pain worsened, I could still help around the house sometimes. Jay and I decided to move, so we had more space, but I wasn't part of the moving process because I couldn't do anything myself. I had to depend on others to move things precious to me. During the move, things were broken and lost. I was so angry, but what could I do besides fuss? The attachment we have to material things can be unhealthy and control our thoughts and actions. Some of the things we consider valuable do not maintain value over time.

We moved about fifteen minutes from Sierra into an apartment with one level. The twins were more independent, and the girls were both in school. The guys looked out for the kids and me. I worked part-time in a salon because I couldn't stand as long, but I still did hair from home. I loved working at *Cutz on the Hill.* It was so much fun; the guys were like brothers to me. So, I always had a job there, no matter how much time passed. I could come back to work.

# CHAPTER 9

## Sisterhood and Surgeries

Sierra and I are spending more time together this spring because my new place is about fifteen minutes from her. When I was recovering, she would catch the bus to the hospital to see me and do my hair. She would say, "just because you're stuck in the bed doesn't mean you can just be looking a mess." When I was released from the hospital and started driving again, we would go to the park with my baby Bunny while Flip and the twins were in school. I sometimes saw her after work because she was on my way home. Sierra worked at TJ Max and met a few friends there. She likes her job, even though she complains now and then.

Although I don't know the full extent, Sierra had her own health issues. She lived in Trinidad for about two years and got into a car accident there. She was okay, but she had lost her front teeth. I drove her to her dentist appointments. Many things happened to her over the years, but we have maintained our close bond. I understood my sister more as I grew older, and we became best friends. I always wanted her to know how much I cared about her even though she was not making good decisions.

I grew up helping to care for all her children, and I felt like they were my babies. After I moved out, I would bring things for my nieces and nephews whenever I visited. Sierra has seven children, and although my family raised them, she loves all of them deeply. And she loves my children just the same, but she clung to my Babygirl. From the first time she held her, they were linked. I don't know what it was. Being a mom has been challenging for Sierra because she had difficulty facing her own identity. She is very fair-skinned, so when people saw all six of us growing up, they often questioned if she was our sister. They would ask why she is so light, and y'all are dark-skinned. The ignorance of people is beyond me. As siblings, we all fought each other, but nobody else could mess with one of us without dealing with all of us. We understood the importance of family, which kept us close.

One day Sierra and I planned a sleepover at her house. Ladybug wanted to come with me. We played card games, and there was a lot of laughing and singing. Fatboy came home earlier than expected, and the twins wanted to be together. "You're gonna get home and not want to drive back here." Sierra rode with me to drop Ladybug off, and the party started again when we got back to her house. We played games on the Wii and sang to Whitney Houston. She is one of Sierra's favorite singers. We stayed up and talked all night.

When I woke up the following day, she was in the other room with her boyfriend laughing and playing around. She came out and talked to me for a few minutes, and my mom called. Ma tried to reach Sierra, but she told me to tell mom she would call her later. Later never comes.

I talked to my mom, went to the bathroom, and heard my name. Why is he calling me like that? There was a disturbing tone in his voice. "Jerre... Jerrrrreee...." I open the bathroom door as he opens the bedroom door. "What's wrong," I say. Your sister; it's something wrong she's not breathing. The next moments move so fast. The ambulance arrives, and Sierra is in and out of consciousness. They ask if she has taken some drugs as if she overdosed. I'm trying to explain that Sierra has been dealing with blood clots. They asked her if she could stand up. *Really? If she can't breathe, how can she stand?* They brought a chair in and stood her up. She fell flat to the floor. I'm holding onto her "Breathe." "Wake up." She's not responding. Now they are rushing. "Oh, this is serious. We have to move." My sister's eyes never opened again. She had one last gasp of air that I felt across my face as I held her.

I couldn't sleep. Every time I closed my eyes. It was like instant replay. How is it that we had such a fantastic time, and Sierra was gone in a blink? Sometimes when we'd talk, I'd become the older sister. I always listened and offered her a different perspective. And when I needed to talk or vent, she was there. She was always one of my biggest cheerleaders. She never discouraged me from trying new things. Sierra just wanted to be loved, and I always showed her how much I loved her. Although she didn't have a perfect life, she's the perfect sister in my eyes. She understood me and my imperfections, and I understood her the same. It was truly a privilege to have her as my sister. She was a beautiful spirit that many misunderstood. I saw her for who she was, and I loved her right where she was. Most of the time, that's all a person needs.

When dealing with life's pain and unfortunate circumstances, some people cope by portraying something they are not. Hiding is a means of protection. I choose to see past it all, while many people only accept what they see on the surface when they meet someone. There are layers of hurt that people walk around holding onto. I peel back the layers to see the people, and I love them from where they are.

I can barely type this because of the tears in my eyes. I'm just now truly grieving. I didn't realize that because of people's judgment, I stopped talking about the trauma I experienced and holding her while she took her last breath. It is crucial to allow yourself to grieve. I didn't; I just tried to make sense of what happened and move on. The pain doesn't go away. In the most unexpected moment, those suppressed feelings resurface.

It took time to realize I had the gift of being with Sierra during her last moments. That's priceless. I hold on to our beautiful night and knowing she was happy. As I reflect, my life perspective is because of my parents and upbringing. Life reflects choices, and I chose to see all the positives. It allowed my eyes to be open to receive even more. I decide to hold tight to the positive, and that same energy is revealed to me. I continue to find the positive in the most negative situation.

If you are dealing with loss or grieving a loved one, I encourage you to take time for yourself. It can be easy to get lost in supporting others through their grief and ignore your feelings. I urge you to tell someone if you've experienced this severe trauma. Be honest about your pain. Allow yourself to cry. When you cry, you release. You must release to heal. The pain may not go away completely, but it will get better. Spend time with those you love and trust. Reach out to them.

The winter after Sierra passed, my back started bothering me again. I had gone from walking fine to asking for help to stand up using my walker. I have developed and maintained a high pain tolerance, so I didn't think much of it at first. After a while, I needed help getting out of bed again.

I was in so much pain Jay took me to the emergency room. I was released, but the pain continued. I kept calling the doctors to find out what was happening. They decided to admit me again. Several tests and images were taken and examined. I distinctly remember getting the spinal tap. They stuck this long needle into my spine to extract fluid samples. The lab results showed if there was any growth from the samples. After a week in the hospital, I was still in excruciating pain. Regardless, doctors sent me home because all the images looked normal, and they could not see what was causing me pain. I pleaded. I couldn't understand how the results showed nothing. As I waited for transport, I realized I'd return home with this excruciating pain. All I could do was cry. Why can't they help me?

My friends and church family always show up for me at crucial times. It's so wonderful to have such great friends who come to help with no questions asked. Although I rarely ask, I told a few church members that I had problems with my back again, and people just showed up. After being released from the hospital, my good friend Janelle came to do my hair. We talked and enjoyed each other's company.

Once she leaves, I am ready to lay down. I'm dosing off, but I can't fall asleep just yet, so I just watch a little TV. Jay is sleeping hard. He had a long day at work. I need to use the bathroom. I drop my legs slowly until my body is in a seated position. I lose control of my legs as I drop them. Immediately I feel a sharp pain shoot through my body. I'm stuck. My legs were hanging off the bed, and I couldn't feel anything but the stabbing pain. "Jay!"

He couldn't hear me. I called him several times before he woke up. "Oh my goodness! What happened? Why are you hanging off the bed? What's wrong? Do you have to use the bathroom?" As I tried to explain, he was calling the ambulance. I am naked and asked him to put some clothes on me. Jay tried, but I was in too much pain to put anything on. "Don't worry about it." He reassured me I would be covered up. When the medics arrived, I was anxious because my pain had calmed down, but I how the pain would return once I moved. Several men came into the bedroom, giving instructions.

I am a plus-sized woman in only my underwear, surrounded by men I don't know. I am lying in the fetal position. They tell me to lay flat on my back. A sharp pain shoots through me as I begin to move, so the medics position me and place me on the board. I cry and scream.

One medic is careless as I am being carried down the hallway and up the stairs. When they put me on the stretcher, the medics guided it out of the room headfirst, and my shoulder slammed against the door frame of my bedroom. I screamed. Once we reached the living room, they turned my feet first. Because of the positioning of the door and the stairs, they angled the stretcher. My feet are out the door. The end of the stretcher hits the railing, the stretcher jolts, and my shoulder bangs against the front door frame. I scream again. The same medic says, "Ma'am, I know it hurts, but please, you have to stop screaming." "Well, if you stop banging her into things, maybe she wouldn't scream," Jay says.

As he is talking, I see my son's face. Ladybug kept my baby girls in their bedroom so they didn't see me that way. I can only imagine what they were going through when they heard me screaming. They finally get me on the stretcher and roll me onto the ambulance, still unclothed as the wind blows. My upper body is exposed to the neighborhood, and I see the neighbors looking from their windows.

The ride to the hospital is just as bumpy as getting onto the ambulance. A sharp pain shoots through my body with every pothole and bump in the road. I was asked questions I couldn't answer because I was in too much pain. Jay answered as many as he could while the hospital contacted my doctor. I got an injection that helped tremendously. I can't remember what they gave me, but it worked. The doctor returned and explained that my surgeon wanted me transported. I dreaded the ride because of how the first ride went, but getting me into the ambulance was smooth. Although the ride was painful, and I still felt the potholes, the medication made it a little more tolerable. When we arrive, a nurse tells me they will send me to get some images so they can figure out what's going on.

They rolled my stretcher into the exam room and gave me an IV with medication that would allow them to see what was going on inside me.

Inside this machine, I hear all types of mechanical noises. "Oh my goodness...I have never seen anything like this in my 30 years". I asked the tech what he saw. With wide eyes, he said, "I'm sorry, ma'am, but I can't discuss that with you. After the doctors review your images, they will talk with you".

I'm nervous now. The nurse gives me medication to keep me comfortable waiting for the doctors. Jay and I were asleep in my hospital room, and we awakened to see about five doctors in my room. *This can't be good.* They said that I needed to be admitted to the hospital, and my surgeon was on his way to talk with me. It only happens in 1% of people, but there is an infection in my spine above and below my existing hardware. Because it went undiagnosed for two months, it destroyed 4 of my vertebrae and 2 of my discs. I had not known that our tissues naturally fight off harmful bacteria in the body. Because metal is not a living organism, harmful bacteria can settle, grow, becoming infected. I would need three surgeries on my back. The first would be to remove the existing hardware and clean out the bone debris; the second was to reconstruct my spine, and the third was to complete the reconstruction. I had to have two reconstruction procedures because they had to install hardware on my spine's inner and outer sides.

During the first surgery, I was cut open on my left side, and they put a cage into my inner spine. I woke up in the ICU to the sound of doctors and nurses speaking about removing the breathing tubes because I became stable and would wake up soon. I was already awake, and the tube was restricting my breathing. I can't catch my breath. I'm trying to get the attention of the doctors and nurses, but they are not looking at me.

I'm waking up again. I can hear Jay talking this time, trying to figure out why I'm strapped to the bed. Even though I listen to him, the doctors still don't realize I'm awake. I can't breathe, and now the machines are noisy because my oxygen levels are decreasing. Then, I see everyone rush in. My heart stopped, and I lost a lot of blood during the first surgery. I was sent to ICU because of the complications, and I needed to be observed for two days until my subsequent surgery. I had tubes everywhere. My vitals were unstable at times. All my lumbar and a portion of my thoracic spine were completely removed.

When I woke up, I saw Jay and the twins. I remember waking up wondering if Ladybug was going to be in there. She said she didn't want to see me like that and wanted to wait until I came home. With tears in her eyes, she said, Mommy, I love you.

I was awake again during my second surgery. I tried to get the surgeon's attention, but they never looked at me. This time, I ended up pulling my tube out, and one of my lungs collapsed. I was out, and when I woke again, I heard Jay arguing with the doctors about me being strapped to the bed. They decided to strap me to the bed so I would not have the same reaction when I woke up. I needed the tube to help me breathe at this point. I had to keep the breathing tube in until the following day. Although my memory is cloudy, I can vividly remember how uncomfortable that tube was, and it's a specific way you must breathe while the tube is inserted. "Breathe with the machine," they said. It's easier said than done.

During my second trip to ICU, I had the worst nurse. She had no sympathy for the amount of pain I was enduring. She was careless, especially when bathing and changing my bedding. One day I couldn't take it anymore. She came to change my bedding, and I couldn't get out of bed or even move at this point. I know I'm not a small woman, so as much as I could. I had to roll to one side for her to start changing my bedding. She would use the sheet to guide me over as far as possible. This lady grabbed the sheet without waiting for me to move with her, and my stitches were snatched. I screamed, of course. She had the nerve to say, "Miss, if you scream like that again, I will not finish changing your bedding."

After a few choice words, I calmed down, and the other nurse came to help her. After rolling to the other side for them to finish up, she aggressively pulled the sheets. Well, it was time for her to go. I went off. I told her to get away from me. I told her she had no business working in this unit and wanted to speak to the head nurse. She began to try and explain herself, but I had dealt with her for a few days, and she clearly didn't like her job. I told her to leave my room and requested a different nurse. After three days, they wanted to move me to a regular room to prep for the final surgery. I couldn't let them put me under again; not so soon anyway. I couldn't explain how I felt; I just didn't feel right. One of my doctors was a true jerk at times. He tried to persuade me to get it done when he wanted, but another doctor reminded me I could choose, so I postponed the next surgery. After a few more days of allowing my body to rest, I felt it was time for my third surgery after two weeks.

My anxiety was high. I was scared but excited because I wanted to walk again. This was all going to help me get there. After a smooth final surgery, the nurses came into my room the following day. "It's time to stand up." I thought I would have some time to rest before getting my body moving. I sat on the bed, and they helped me slide to the edge. Now on 3, push up with your legs. I'm trying. Nothing is happening but pain. Try again. *How can I do this if I can't feel my legs?* I tried two more times, and then I got very dizzy. My blood count was low, and I needed a transfusion; two more blood bags.

The following day the nurses came into my room. "It's time to try and stand again." They told me not to focus on the lack of feeling but just push up out of my seat and stand. Later, when my family visited me, I used the bathroom and did not want to wait for the nurse. After some struggle, I stood again. All four of my children came to see me, and their faces showed hope and possibility. Still, I didn't have feelings in my legs, and there was no guarantee of full recovery. Though it was a true struggle, I remained faithful; the pain was extreme, but it was less than the pain I was in before the surgery, and each day improved. I was in inpatient rehabilitation for about six weeks, maybe more. They have me on so much pain medication that parts of my memories are clouded. I won't forget moments, and they stick with me always.

There is one moment that I can't forget because of my baby girl, Bunny. She was a light when my world was so dark. Learning how to walk again was very uncomfortable and painful. Here comes this little person with the biggest personality during my therapy session. Her smile warmed my heart and eased the pain. Don't get me wrong, all four of my babies have a special place in my heart. I have a special relationship with each of them. They empower me to be the best me possible. Bunny would walk with me and hold onto the front of my walker. I was having a hard time one visit, and I said I couldn't do it anymore. She came over and said, "Mommy, I can help you. I can show you how to walk." As tears came to my eyes, her little legs took one step and then another. "See, I can show you. Come on; I will help you." Holding on to the front of my walker, she guided my steps. Her tiny voice said, "now lift your foot and do the other one. That's it, mommy, you got it." Have you ever taught your children, and then they turn around to teach you the same things? As a parent, you would never think about that. To experience a child teaching you or guiding you through your life journey is the most incredible thing.

I've encountered many doctors over the past twelve years dealing with my spinal issues. Listening to the doctors is one thing, but we should always look deeper into our bodies and be determined to find and own our health and wellness. Doctors lean on their degree or license to prove they know how to repair my body. There is no blueprint to solving living with chronic pain. For everyone who lives in pain, they know medication is not always a solution. Getting creative by combining exercise, natural supplements, and medications will bring you to a place of comfort. Sometimes switching up the combination and troubleshooting the combination will help.

It is best to learn about your symptoms and gain a deeper understanding of your body is best. Communicate constantly with the doctors and people around you. Ask lots of questions and do your research because sometimes they don't give you all the information that will benefit you. Hospitals support your healing but unfortunately, because there are many sick people in that environment, you sometimes leave with more than you entered. Doctors don't know you the way you know yourself. You must be your own advocate.

I realized I needed doctors who think outside the box with treatment. Multiple surgeries affect the whole body, every area that has to be cut through to get to the damaged area. Scar tissue affects the nerves and muscles. After seven surgeries, can you imagine the havoc it wreaks on my body? Since my bones are very dense, all three surgeries took over 10 hours. My body felt terrible.

My nurse and therapist encouraged me to get up, and I would feel better. That didn't make sense to me at first. *I'm hurting, and you want me to walk around.* There is no way I'm getting out of bed feeling this type of pain. This was when I first experienced walking through my pain. Getting out of bed caused pain to shoot through my legs. Sharp stabbing pain and I don't think that can explain well. Putting pressure on my feet made it worse. The nurse helped me. She said, "Do you trust me." "I didn't have a choice but to trust her. "Just focus on moving your legs. It's going to get better." At that moment, I had to dig deeper than ever. It hurt, but I only focused on wanting to walk again. *Just move your legs* is what I kept saying to myself. As I took each step, it was so painful at first, but after I got to the hallway, I could feel a bit less sharp shooting pain in my legs.

Heading home from rehabilitation was no walk in the park. My relationship with my husband was rocky, and we had bills stacked up. Jay was stressed. I was worried because the kids didn't have the parenting system they were accustomed to. I came home with a pic line on my arm. This is an IV for extended use. It allowed me to get the liquid form of antibiotics. I had a nurse and therapist come weekly to work with me. Learning my new normal was so hard. I wanted to go to work and drive my kids around to events. If I could just be a mom again, I would be happy. I just wanted to walk without assistance. Soon I was doing it, building my strength.

# CHAPTER 10

# Getting to Know Me

I separated from Jay twice before deciding to get a divorce. Our ten years together were not all bad. For a while, I enjoyed our family dynamic of being spiritually grounded. Taking the family to church was very important to him and still is today. Jay is a family man but enjoys his (playtime) downtime. During our marriage, I felt playtime should be less of a priority because we were still trying to build a life together. An issue that kept coming up was his interactions with other women. I cannot say that he cheated on me, but his constant flirting was frustrating. He didn't view it like that whenever I would point it out to him.

We are family-oriented, but our upbringings differed, so we thought differently about the family's needs. I prepared for the future, while Jay functioned only in the present. I thought we would make it work, being raised so differently. Jay is the youngest of six on his dad's side, but he did not grow up in his household. Although he has a big family, it was mostly him and his mother. I grew up learning how to care for and consider my siblings. He was not required to do that because it was just him and his mother. It was his world. As we got older and our family grew, I noticed our relationship suffered because of our differences. In our downtime, I liked working on our future. Jay worked hard, so in his downtime, he wanted to chill. At some point, we both became self-absorbed and stuck in our ways. This caused a major clash.

The actual day I decided to leave permanently was February 28th. A month prior, I sat down with him and explained that I needed him to be more present in the home. I had just had my seventh back surgery, and I couldn't handle the stress of our relationship and take care of myself plus the kids. We argued about everything. I was always irritated. Even his snoring made me mad. The months leading up to my leaving were very toxic. I had to choose between my relationship and myself. In my mind, something had to go. It wasn't going to be myself, and it by no means would be the kids. I begged him to stop going out so much. I begged him to be more present with the kids. I told him the kids and I were leaving if I didn't see a change in the next month. I think he had already given up. He had two preteens, two toddlers, and a sick wife. His wife, who handled most of the household things, was no good to him in the capacity he was used to.

I learned that I needed to care for myself to return to caring for my children. The kids and I moved in with my brother Donnell. He didn't want me to go anywhere else. Donnell has always been there for my kids as if they were his own. He is such an amazing supportive brother. Living with him was great. He and his wife welcomed the kids and me.

I continued to get on my feet and lived with my mom for a while. The kids were happy to be with their grandmother, and I realized I was an emotional wreck. Anyone talking to me about my marriage, the divorce, or the decisions I made for myself fell on deaf ears. I couldn't hear anything anyone was saying to me. These were two long years of my life. I was still recovering from all my surgeries and trying to take care of my children. Then on top of everything, Jay was not present. That wasn't a surprise at all, but that didn't make it less hurtful. He was busy with work and friends and the motorcycle club. He would get the girls three weekends out of the month, and they stayed with his mom for two. So really, he only spent one weekend a month with them. I couldn't do anything about it, and it frustrated me.

Living with my mom allowed me to give her what she had given me. She has physical limitations that she is overcoming. At times she is uncomfortable with people seeing her function like this. She deals with a lot of pain. I encouraged her. I'm helping her to understand that I know where she is. I'm happy that she has now experienced a better quality of life through renovations to help her move through her house better with the walker. She has a little bit of movement on her own. One of the biggest things she wanted was some of her independence back. She has that now. God orders my steps to grow me and serve people on my journey. Everyone I've helped along my journey has pushed me deeper into my purpose.

After our divorce was final, we had a conversation. We talked in the elevator, and we apologized to one another. Jay apologized for not being there for me the way I needed him to. I apologized for my reactions to what he was doing and not doing. We realized we both could have done things differently. If nothing else I learned from all I went through with him, you must love a person for who they are. Don't try to change them. If they change, it must be their choice. We, as little girls, sometimes grow up with this image in our heads of what a man is supposed to be. The reality is if you focus on growing yourself, a man that loves you unconditionally will change. He will change because you have loved him despite his imperfections.

Today I call Jay my friend. He is not perfect, and neither am I. We can talk and laugh with each other. We both know that we are better as friends. Our history cannot be forgotten, and we both agree that it made us a better version of ourselves. As Jay reflects, he says most of his choices had a lot to do with how bad my health got. While that's no excuse, it's his truth. It was a lot for him to manage himself with four kids and a very sick wife. He understood that my expectations for him were high because of how I viewed my father. Jay felt like he didn't fit the bill. Since we married so young and I already had twins, we both brought a lot into our marriage and learned so much on the journey. Nobody wants to go through a divorce, but for us, it was better that we didn't stay together for our children. They did not deserve to stay in a toxic living space. Although my children have both parents fully involved and we are successful co-parents, I believe it takes much more effort to maintain and balance social and emotional support because we have separated households.

I appreciate Jay's willingness to care for my twins. When the twins were eight years old, I reconnected with DJ. He agreed to a paternity test. He is indeed their biological father. He has continued being in and out of their lives from that point on. I understand that he has his problems, but I'm still frustrated that he is a good person when he comes around. It's the absent version of him that pisses me off. I wish he would snap out of where ever his mind is. Sometimes I wonder if it's better he didn't show up. His absence still has a lasting impact on them. It's easy to move on from a dad you don't see, but when they see him occasionally, and he is still not there for them, I think that hurts worse.

# CHAPTER 11

# Self Care

Life is what some of my clients say about their hair; there are kinks, tangles, and knots. The kinks are the life changes. The tangles I compare to the relationships with not only people but things. It's like a tug of war to get the tangles out, and sometimes it's the dead hair that causes it, so people or things that we don't need will tug and pull on us, but then eventually, we release it (like dead hair from our scalp).

After a long journey to emotional and physical recovery, I can say I am on the other side of it. These days I'm walking with no assistance. I trained my body to return to my passion for doing hair. I took an opportunity to return to the shop, and my career took off. I thrived as both a stylist and assistant manager. I was so motivated, and I wanted more for myself. Faniesha suggested I inquire about a position in a corporate salon. Not only was I hired, but I earned the manager position. I am now part of a community of like-minded people who support me in reaching my goals. I'm making new relationships and understanding the importance of evaluating all relationships so that it's always a healthy balance. I have learned to create time for myself. Now, I know the importance of balancing business and personal. I care for myself and am my best self in all situations.

My children are all doing great. The twins have graduated from high school. Ladybug is a thriving young adult career building, socializing, dating, and enjoying her 20s. Fatboy had his share of obstacles; I supported him as he figured things out. I am now a grandmother, and Fatboy is a family man.

I cut up my baby doll's hair when I was a little girl. With minimal supplies, I can achieve any look. My talent comes from my mom; as my girls have gotten older, they have the talent. Each of us is born with a gift, and gifts may go unnoticed. On the other hand, talent is an ability that is cultivated through hard work. My gift is empathizing with others and leadership. My talent is the art of hair, but I can say this is a gift because I could look at a picture and figure out how to achieve the look at a young age. Every chapter of my life has given me a clear understanding of my purpose. At a young age, my baby girls could see the gift of hair art in them. Bunny created her first braid at 3yrs old. Flip, at the age of 14, Flip has fostered her talent and is teaching herself techniques and learning things from her older sister, Ladybug, an amazing stylist. Seeing how the skills have grown even more with each generation is gratifying. My children need me, but I need them as well. We motivate, love, and encourage each other.

I was in a car accident that wasn't my fault. This accident became a catalyst that helped me move closer to my purpose. I struggled to pay all my bills, and the accident made things very tight. Complaining gets me nowhere, but coming up with a game plan and executing by any means necessary. I picked up new clients at the shop, and some old timeless clients returned after losing contact for a few years. I had one more payment, and I would finally have caught up on all payments. I communicated with the rental office and ensured I was still in good standing. I was still evicted, BUT GOD. My steps are ordered, and he will carry me if I don't move. What I prayed for and the answer I received wasn't the answer I wanted. *Did you catch it?*

Today I look forward to smashing all the goals I have set for myself and my family unit. My children and I have a home, and my grandchild is precious. I am well-rested and ready to start my day. Nothing could stop my flow. A few months back, I was almost caught up on my bills from a car accident. I had bills due, but I've gained a perspective on viewing this type of obstacle. I took my time leaving out, which is very unusual for me. I love to get to the shop before my clients arrive. I didn't have an early client, so I did some housework and talked on the phone a bit. It was time to leave out. I gather my belongings to take with me to work. My granddaughter and her mom were in the house. My son was on his way home but hadn't made it back. I kiss my granddaughter goodbye.

I'm waiting for my car's engine to heat up and observing my surroundings. The car is heated, and I am ready to pull off, but my spirit feels uneasy. I sit for a few more minutes, and a car pulls up. I look across the complex and then across from my building. A few moments later, a large group of people and the sheriffs come out. I get out of my car, watching them go into another building. They walked towards my building, and saw them heading up the stairs. I called out to them, asking which apartment they were going to. With tears in my eyes, I try to explain and show them my payments and tell them I just spoke with the lady in the office. She said my account is current and in good standing. "Ma'am, this is a judgment for consistent late payment. There's nothing I can do". They allow me to go back into the apartment to gather important belongings. At this point, my son is home and trying to help resolve the issue.

Once again, a kink enters my life. This time, I have learned to call on my day ones to help me. I stood there and watched as they tossed out my furniture. Things were breaking and shattering. When my friend Clint came, I knew everything would be ok. I sat in Clint's truck, and he helped me map out a plan of action to figure out where I would live. My brother brought me a UHaul, and Jay picked up the girls. My girls were confused and sad, but they tried to keep it together. I could see how disturbed they were to see all our belongings thrown out like trash on the curb. My neighbor was going through the same thing, and her grandchildren were crying badly. It was cold out. I had so much help moving my belongings that I was able to bless the other family who had no money or family to help them get off the street.

There's always a positive in a negative if only you allow yourself to see it. God allowed me to lose my apartment to bless the family next door. Little did I know that the blessing in my life was yet to come. Later that day, I went to work, trying not to think about being homeless. My son was approved for an apartment and asked me to move in. I loved being with my son and his family. Although his girlfriend and I were not besties, we had some nice moments and really meaningful conversations. Fatboy is smart, strong, and takes good care of me. When everything seemed so dark, he brought light into my life. As I move into my purpose, life has gotten challenging at times. My son always calls in the darkest moments and gives me a word.

There's chatter at the shop constantly about coronavirus. I'm not watching much news, but this made me tune in. The owner comes into the shop, and we have a management meeting, and it's decided that we are shutting down completely. At this point, I've lost my apartment, and my baby girls have moved in with dad full time, so I feel like I list them too. Now my job is shutting down. They say everything happens in 3's. As a teenager, it was Bell's palsy, corrective surgery on my leg, and sexual assault. As an adult, the loss of my dad, Big Granma, then being diagnosed with spinal stenosis. Then the loss of my ability to walk, the loss of my sister, and the loss of my marriage. God uses those bad things for the ultimate, lasting good. God sometimes allows trials and tribulations to mold us and move us toward what he has planned for our life.

Perseverance is not for the faint of heart. It takes total determination and dedication to follow through despite the inherent obstacles. You may be discouraged by family, friends, or your circumstances. It can be uncomfortable recognizing and assessing where you truly are. Being complacent about where you are should never be an option. You have a purpose. Regardless of your life stage, remember that progress is constant forward motion.

There are some things in life you will never truly heal from, but through writing this book, I learned that healing is a process. Everything that has happened in your life affects who you are today, but you can choose if it will keep you down or elevate you. I believe healing happens when you push through the pain, whether it's emotional or physical. We all endure some pain in life, and we can endure much more than we think. I choose to be anchored in Christ to power through any life obstacle. I stand firm in the belief that He is the author and finisher. When it is too dark to see, He is the light.

Today with God's grace I am able to stand behind the chair. I help my clients through the kinks of life and hair.

As I heal clients' scalps I also have the pleasure of helping them work through life's obstacles. My teenagers, I truly enjoy talking with them. They are at a tricky and the unpredictable stage Just like curly hair, you never know what to expect. Creating beautiful hair art is my talent. My gift is to inspire people using my own life journey as a tool. As I stand behind the chair I meet so many wonderful people and listening to their personal life challenges allows me to encourage, motivate, and inspire them to never give up.

# Journal Entries

My favorite style to create is the two-strand flat twist updo. It's my signature style. Two small sections of hair are gathered between my fingertips. With systematic movements, the two sections crossover, pick up just a little more hair and cross it again. My left hand has to sync with my right hand to create the perfect twist. The hair is grabbed up and crossed over, creating a flat twist with the end result of a beautiful rope-like hairdo that can be dressed up or down.

Self-reliance means having confidence in and exercising one's own powers of judgment. Someone said to me, "Can you just be soft like a female?" I had to meditate on this statement. Most recently, I've been rethinking this concept of self-reliance and independence. Dependence is when you are in the mode of receiving information and learning. You rely upon people and haven't stepped into your own agency. Interdependence is mutually dependent; reliant on one another. I think interdependence comes when true self-awareness is present for both people. I've now come to realize it's ok to be interdependent and dependent. Knowing what stage you are in takes wisdom and spiritual awareness. Those you rely on have a significant influence on your future.

Working in a salon, I watched other women take clients. As an assistant, I wondered if I could put my skills to work. I watched time after time people come in asking for braids. I didn't want just to sit around waiting anymore, so one day when a client came in for braids, I decided sitting around was no longer an option. Sometimes you must see the opportunity and take it. Life presents you with opportunities, and you either take them or stay in the same place. Seize every opportunity and make it great. Our lives can be defined by the opportunities that we take or miss. It is up to us to decide.

In my current shop, we function as a team. The shop atmosphere reflects family because we all work together to bring joy to our clients. From the moment the door is unlocked in the morning to when we are cleaning up and ready to head home, we all thrive on one another's energy. One by one we come in with the music playing. We greet and fuel each other with feelings of joy and excitement for the day. Our clients are like our cousins coming to visit. We all look forward to seeing our cousins and exchanging our life stories. Catching up on what's happened since the last time we saw each other. We are individual stylists and barbers with a common goal to achieve the client's desired look and great vibes during their service. It's a family affair!

In life, we must move systematically through obstacles. Our character is developed by facing and overcoming obstacles. Fear and perfection are two of the biggest obstacles we face in life. On the other side of fear are some of our most gratifying life experiences. Perfectionism leads to procrastination, and procrastination leads to goals not being achieved. Create a system that helps you face challenges like fear and perfectionism. As the system keeps getting used, it will no longer be necessary.

My clients come in and may have good or bad days. They may be dealing with some life obstacles or have a life win that I hear about. I can be so engaged with my clients that I can feel that emotion as they tell their life stories. I enjoy the relationships I build with them. Each one is different, and some have become like family. Ms. Francis is a fun-loving spicy woman, and her daughter Val is my client. Everyone knows her when she enters the shop, and we all have major respect for her.

I look forward to her visit to the shop. We exchanged casual conversations with lots of laughter. One day, a guy came in telling us that one of our clients fell outside and asked for the owner. I was concerned, so I followed him outside. It was her, Ms. Francis, lying face-first on the ground. We rushed over to aid her. Our shop is in a busy shopping center, it was at the peak of the day. Many people were standing around wanting to know if she was ok. Her mouth was bleeding, and the position of her body was very concerning. I was worried. Wondering if she hit her head or damaged her mouth and hoped she didn't break anything during the fall. Nate called the ambulance and all we could do was wait. She laid face-first on the ground. I sat beside her on the ground until the ambulance arrived as she lay there. I didn't want her to feel uncomfortable in an already acquired situation. I sat down and rested my hand on her back to let her know she was not alone. The owner, Nate, talks about me sitting on the ground next to Ms. Francis to this day. Val was truly grateful for us being with her mother at that moment. I stopped working to care for the client and gained a great friendship.

These are moments that bring me joy. Bringing people joy through the art of hair is such a wonderful thing. What's even better is the family connections that are generated.

The tangles of life can be smoothed out using these three simple steps:

A…Assess
B…Be ok
C…Commit

Assess where you are. Understanding that this is not your finish line.

Be ok with what you have assessed. Creating goals and a plan of execution.

Committing to the process. Understanding that it is the journey to reach the goals that matter most.

# About The Author

Jerre Northington is a mother of four and grandmother of two. She is building her career as a leader and manager at N'style Hair Grooming. She is the general manager and assistant to the owner. Where they serve our community with hair grooming services, food donations, health and wellness education, etc.

Jerre has battled emotional and physical pain. From early motherhood to the loss of her dad and physical health she created JWNaturals. JWNATURALS LLC is Jerre's brand where she uses the art of hair as a tool to inspire, motivate, and encourage clients through life obstacles.

Her motto is, "Inspiring Beauty From The Inside Out".

Jerre has a 24-year career that stems from passion for the health of the scalp and hair. As her career developed she gained a wealth of knowledge about internal health and mental health. With deeper studies, she connected the two. The health of the hair can be disturbed by internal imbalances. This is where her passion shifted to helping clients understand beauty from the inside out.

www.ingramcontent.com/pod-product-compliance
Lightning Source LLC
La Vergne TN
LVHW090532110826
845146LV00003B/1074

* 9 7 9 8 2 1 8 0 7 0 2 3 6 *